BOO

LONDON

Kingfisher Books, Grisewood & Dempsey Ltd,
Elsley House, 24–30 Great Titchfield Street,
London W1P 7AD

First published in this edition in 1988
by Kingfisher Books
Part of the material in this book was originally
published in hardcover in 1981 as *Discovering London*
by Kingfisher Books/Ward Lock Ltd

Copyright © Kingfisher Books Ltd 1981, 1988

All rights reserved. No part of this publication
may be reproduced, stored in a retrieval system or
transmitted by any means, electronic, mechanical,
photocopying or otherwise, without the prior
permission of the publisher.

BRITISH LIBRARY CATALOGUING IN PUBLICATION DATA
Marks, Graham
  Pocket book of London.
  1. London (England) – Description – 1981 –
  – Guide-books – Juvenile literature
  I. Title II. Maynard, Chris III. Powell, Anton
  914.21'04858   DA679
ISBN 0 86272 328 0

Edited & designed by 2ems Publishing Partnership
Colour section designed by Ben White
Cover design by David Jefferis
Phototypeset by Southern Positives and Negatives (SPAN)
Printed and bound in Italy by Vallardi Industrie Grafiche, Milan

BOOK OF
LONDON

G. MARKS, C. MAYNARD & A. POWELL

KINGFISHER BOOKS

Contents

Chapter 1: **Getting Around** 8–9
　　　　　　The Tube 10–11
　　　　　　Buses. 12–13
　　　　　　Railways. 14–15
　　　　　　Sightseeing 16–17

Chapter 2: **Royal London**. 18–19
　　　　　　The Palace. 20–21
　　　　　　The Tower. 22–23
　　　　　　Westminster. 24–25
　　　　　　Horse Guards 26–27
　　　　　　Other Palaces. 28–29

Chapter 3: **Waterways**. 30–31
　　　　　　Exploring the River 32–33
　　　　　　A Trip on the River 34–35
　　　　　　The Trip Continues. 36–37
　　　　　　Canals. 38–39

Chapter 4: **The City**. 40–41
　　　　　　The City at Work 42–43
　　　　　　Legal London 44–45
　　　　　　A Citywalk/1 46–47
　　　　　　A Citywalk/2 48–49

Chapter 5: **Sinister London**. 50–51
　　　　　　Child Thieves. 52–53
　　　　　　A Grim Death 54–55
　　　　　　Beheaded!. 56–57

Chapter 6:	**A Rainy Day**	58–59
	Monsters and Mummies .	60–61
	Pictures That Tell a Story	62–63
	Little Museums	64–65
	Crowns and Crosses	66–67
	Shop Windows...........	68–69
Chapter 7:	**Outdoor London**	70–71
	London Wildlife	72–73
	Zoo Life	74–75
	Street Markets	76–77
	Secret Railway	78–79
Chapter 8:	**Things to Do**.............	80–81
	Sports to Watch	82–83
	Sports to Try	84–85
	Unusual Activities	86–87
Chapter 9:	**In a Year**.................	88–91
Chapter 10:	**Places to Visit**	92–181
Index..........................		182–191

1: Getting Around

Planning a visit to London can be almost as much fun as the visit itself. It's a good idea to use a map to find your way. Maps are easy to understand, but lots of people never learn to use them. They have to rely on others for directions. Some of the easiest maps to use are the London 'A to Z' and the 'Streetfinder'.

> Number 10 Downing Street is the official 'home' of the Prime Minister. A policeman is on duty day and night. He lets people stand at the end of the street and watch visitors come and go.

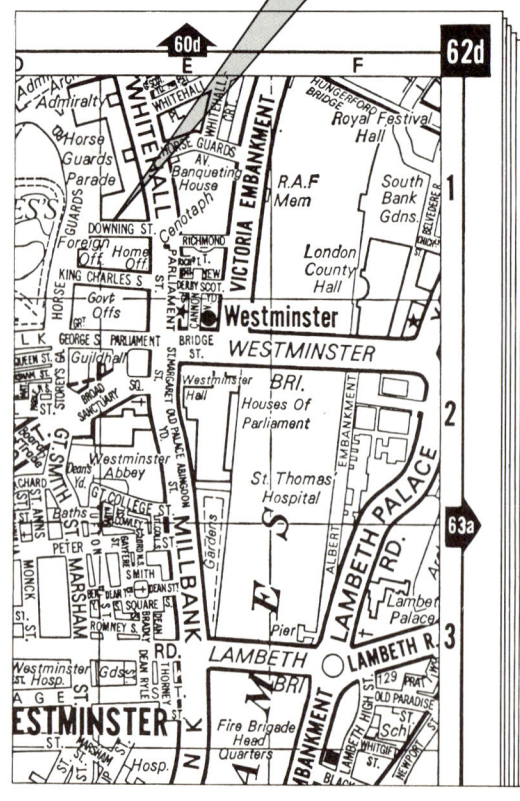

▶ If using the 'A to Z', first look up the name of the street you want at the back of the book. If you want Downing Street (where the Prime Minister lives) the index may say, 'Downing St. SW1 – 1E 62d'. The 'SW1' means the street is in the postal district of South-West One.

To locate the street on the map itself, look at page '62d'. Then use the reference '1E' to find where on the page Downing Street is. First look *down* the numbered rows, then *along* the lettered rows until you find the square where '1' and 'E' match. Within this square you will find Downing Street.

Lost and Found

If you lose your way in London, don't worry. There are lots of people who can help you. Postmen, taxi drivers, milkmen, traffic wardens and police are good people to ask. Part of their job is to know the names of nearby streets. Local shops are often very helpful too. When you are going somewhere new, look out for unusual landmarks. It is fairly easy to remember things like a crane on a building site, a broken concrete lamp-post, or a house with no roof.

Taxi Driver

Traffic Warden

▲ If you have to phone someone but have run out of money, simply go into a phone box and dial 100. Tell the operator your name and the name and number of the person you are ringing and say you want to 'reverse the charges'. The operator rings and asks if the person will pay for the call. If they say yes you can then talk.

Postman

People to Ask

If you are lost, the best people to try are taxi drivers. They have to pass a test called 'The Knowledge', for which they learn central London by heart. If you can't find one, remember that every phone booth has its location printed on a small card – you can then find where you are on a map.

Policeman

The Tube

London's underground railway is known as the 'Tube'. Much of it runs through immensely strong tunnels which are as deep as 67 metres below the ground.

The Tube was built for fast travel. Transport in the streets is often slow, but below ground Tube trains have the tunnels to themselves. This means that during rush hours, at the busiest stations, a train pulls in every two minutes. In the course of one year, more people pass through Oxford Circus station than live in the whole of Britain.

▶ Tube trains run on electricity. There are four rails in the track. The wheels of the train run along one set of rails, the other carries the electricity. A special part of the train makes contact with the electrified rails; the current then passes into the engine of the train and makes it go. No one, except railway engineers, must ever touch the middle rail, for the electric current can kill. The cutaway drawing shows Bond Street Station.

At many stations you can ask for a free map which shows every station and line of the Tube system. Often the station nearest to you is on a different line from the station you want to go to. Look at the map to find the spot where the two lines meet. There you can change lines. Signs inside the station will tell you how to reach the platform you need to get to.

The men and women of London Transport work hard to make the Tube safe. If trains are not carefully controlled, they might plough into each other in the tunnels, so along each line there are signal lights. When a train has just passed a light, it turns red. This tells the driver of the next train not to go through yet. If a driver made a mistake and drove past, the train would stop automatically.

On the Victoria Line the trains are almost completely automatic. A machine tells them how fast to go and where to stop at each platform. The trains still have a driver in the cab, but he does not need to control them between stations, though passengers feel safer if they know there is always a driver in front.

In Victoria Line stations there is a television to help the driver. The screen is near the driver's end of the platform and shows the driver what is happening at the far end of his long train.

◀ On the most up-to-date lines trains go especially fast. As they approach a station, the air they push in front of them makes a howling noise. From the platform you can see their headlights approaching.

Buses

The best way to start exploring London is to travel by bus. You can get a bus map free from main Tube and Bus stations. Find a route that goes near you, and see whether you would like to explore all the way to its terminus. When you get there, a bus with the same number will take you back.

Going by bus can be a very friendly way to travel. Sometimes conductors know a lot about their route. They may be glad to answer a question or two about where the bus is going. But when the bus is full, the conductor has a lot of work to do, so save your questions for when there aren't many passengers.

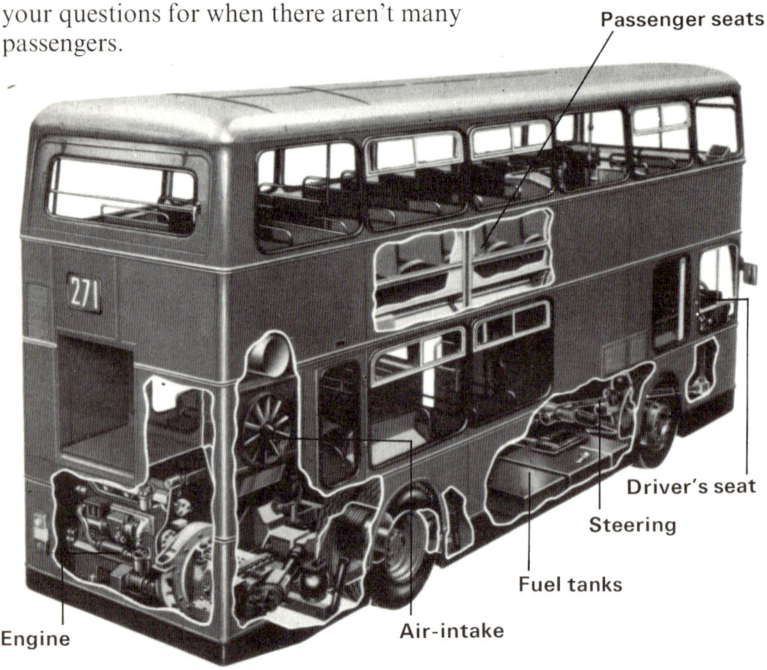

Passenger seats

Driver's seat

Steering

Fuel tanks

Engine

Air-intake

▲ The main weight of a double-decker bus is carried very low down. This means that the bus has little chance of tipping over, even when it is full and going round tight corners.

▲ The original London bus was a horse-drawn double-decker.

▲ London bus tickets are printed by the conductor as he turns the ticket-machine handle.

View from the Top

Sit on the top deck, if you can. There you can look over walls and bridges – and see gardens, railways, canals and much more. When a bus is nearly full, only a few passengers can get on at each stop. You may hear the conductor say something like 'one inside and three on top!' – odd, you think, upstairs is inside too. The reason may be that early horse-drawn buses in the 1800s did not have a roof on the top deck. This made the buses lighter and easier for the horses to pull, although passengers were left in the open air. Only the passengers on the lower deck were inside the bus, and so only the bottom deck came to be called 'inside'.

No one is allowed to stand on the top deck when the bus is moving except the conductor. This is a safety measure, because although buses are designed not to topple over, even if something hits them, if a crowd of people stood upstairs, the bus would be top-heavy.

The Flying Bus

Bus drivers are highly trained and experienced, but in the 1950s, one met a problem no amount of training would have helped. He was driving over Tower Bridge, and had almost reached the middle where the two arms of the bridge join. Suddenly the bridge began to open by mistake.

As the arms moved apart, the bus driver could see the river below and he had to decide very quickly what to do. He could have braked hard, to stop the bus, but then the passengers would have been thrown forward and some could have been injured. Instead, the driver skilfully accelerated. His bus literally flew through the air, jumping the gap from one arm of the bridge to the other so that he could drive it to safety on the other side.

Railways

London's main-line railway stations lie in a ring around the middle of the city. From Paddington trains go to the west of England; from Euston, St Pancras and King's Cross trains go to the north. From Waterloo and Victoria, trains leave for the south coast. There is no main railway line which goes right across London; to get from one station to another you have to take a bus or Tube. The reason is that when the stations were built in the 1800s they were owned by rival railway companies who often disliked each other and certainly didn't want their lines to be connected.

▲ A map of the main railway stations of London. Most are connected by the Circle Line.

◀ From the outside, St Pancras Station looks as if someone had dropped a fairyland castle into London.

Most of London's railway stations were built in Queen Victoria's time (she reigned from 1837 to 1901). People sometimes call this period 'The Railway Age'. With no competition from motor cars, the railway companies made huge profits and could afford to build fine, imposing stations. But because lines to central London were expensive the stations ended up circling the centre.

The most interesting of these stations is St Pancras. It is built of red bricks that are typical of the 19th century and which make it look more like a cathedral than a railway station. The building has tall spires on top, and high pointed windows. Inside the station, there is a cast iron and glass roof over the platforms. The Victorians loved this style of building because it reminded them of the great churches of the Middle Ages.

Inside a Station

Some stations seem to specialize in certain kinds of travellers. At Paddington you'll see families going on holiday to the west of England. At Victoria there's a lot of traffic to and from the Continent. To help foreign travellers many station signs are in French and German. At Waterloo you can often see young men with very short hair, carrying large suitcases. They are soldiers and sailors from the army camps and naval docks of southern England, though they do not wear uniforms when travelling.

Behind the scenes at all the major mainline stations are the men, women and computers which control the journeys of the countless freight and passenger trains using the railway network. Through a complex electronic system each area controller knows the exact location of every train he is responsible for, and he can clear them through via the signals you can see alongside the track.

▲ The inside of a big station is like a small town. Here you can find shops, hotels, banks and restaurants.

▼ Two big expresses wait side by side in Paddington Station. They run to the west of the country.

Sightseeing

If you would like to join a group to see London, there are several ways to go about it. Special sightseeing buses are run by London Transport. You don't have to book in advance, and the buses run seven days a week. They leave every hour on the hour from Marble Arch, Piccadilly Circus and Grosvenor Gardens close to Victoria Station.

None of these tour buses has a guide on board, but if you would like to ride on a bus where there is a commentary about the places you pass, you should go to Victoria Coach Station. London Transport runs tours from here, although you must book a place in advance.

Ordinary red London buses are also good for exploring. With special tour tickets, which do not cost much, you can travel wherever London buses run, wandering over 2750 kilometres on 300 routes anywhere in the London area.

A trip along the Thames on a sunny day is like having a short holiday. There are many boat tours you can take. They leave from Tower Pier, Charing Cross and Westminster Pier in central London, and travel down river as far as Greenwich and up river to Hampton Court.

At Heathrow Airport, you can spend hours at the Spectators' Roof Gardens between Terminals 1 and 2. Here you can go plane-spotting, or simply watch aircraft land and take off. The observation gallery is on the roof of the building. There are also telescopes for people to use as they look at the swarming activity of one of the world's biggest airports. You can take the Piccadilly Line there direct from the centre of town.

▲ For those who want a lot of culture in a little time, why not look out for the Culture Bus! There are 37 places that it stops around London, and for a flat fee you can hop on and off as many times as you like.

▼ A wonderful way to see the sights and colours of London is to take a ride in the open-top tour bus run by London Transport. It covers about 32 kilometres, and passes many of the main places of interest as it loops through the centre of town.

Guided Tours

There are dozens of guided tours to take around London. On the Tower of London tours you can talk to the Yeomen Warders, or Beefeaters, in their old-fashioned uniforms.

Many museums have special tours and lectures. Don't be afraid to join one of these tours and ask the guide questions about anything you notice.

A very good way to learn about London is to go on a guided outdoor walk. An organization called London Walks arranges many of them and they show you where exciting and sometimes shocking things happened in the past. One walk is about the Great Plague and Fire of the 1660s. You can see where plague victims are buried, and where the Great Fire of London started. Other walks visit Roman ruins, or the places where Jack the Ripper carried out his terrible murders in the East End.

◄ The Thames is a fascinating river to watch on its journey through London. In the west it passes leafy suburbs with splendid riverside homes. In central London it flows by the Houses of Parliament, then rows of City skyscrapers and the Tower of London. To the east of the City, the crumbling docks and warehouses have been restored and made into new offices and homes. The modern port has moved downstream.

2: Royal London

The kings and queens of England have lived in London for hundreds of years, since before William the Conqueror. Evidence of past and present royalty can be found everywhere.

Since the 1400s, England has been ruled by several different royal families. The Welsh Tudors were on the throne from 1485 to 1603. King Henry VIII, and his daughter Elizabeth I, were both Tudors. In 1603, the Scottish king, James Stuart, became King of England. His son, Charles I, was so unpopular that he had his head cut off by order of Parliament. The next family after the Stuarts were the Hanoverians. The first king was George I. He was German and could hardly speak English. Today's Queen Elizabeth II is his great-great-great-great-great-great-great-granddaughter.

▼ Every year the Queen comes to the Houses of Parliament. She sits on a throne in the House of Lords and makes a speech. The Queen's speech tells people what the Government wants to do in the following year. But it is the Government, not the Queen, that writes the speech.

The Queen's Powers
Until the 1800s the kings and queens of Britain were very powerful indeed and played a big part in ruling the country. Nowadays the Queen no longer has these powers, instead it is the government that runs the country. The Queen is still called the 'Head of State', however some people, called republicans, believe that even this job is too important for a person who is not elected. They would like to do without the royal family entirely.

▲ You will often see a badge saying 'E II R' in London. It stands for 'Elizabeth the Second Regina'. *Regina* is the Latin word for Queen. A good place to find the royal badge is on post boxes. On old ones you can find the badges of earlier rulers. The badge 'G VI R' stands for 'George the Sixth Rex'. (*Rex* means king.) He was the present Queen's father and reigned until 1952. A few very old post boxes have the letters 'VR' on them. These stand for 'Victoria Regina'. If you find a box with her badge on it you can be almost sure it was made in the 1800s.

▼ The battered post boxes of London are a record of the past if you know what they mean. You can get a rough idea of their age from the ruler's initials on the side.

The Palace

Just about everyone must have heard of Buckingham Palace. It is the most famous of the Queen's many homes. It stands behind high railings at the end of a street called The Mall. If you walk along The Mall you can easily tell if the Queen is in the Palace that day. If she is, the royal flag flies from the roof.

Behind the railings of the palace stand the Palace guards. They wear red tunics and tall black fur hats called 'busbies'. In the 1800s, this type of headgear was worn in battle to frighten the enemy as it made soldiers look taller and fiercer. Nowadays if the guards go into combat they don't wear this uniform. In the modern army they dress in camouflage clothes so that the enemy cannot see them easily. The old-style

▼ Each regiment of guards has a different pattern of buttons on its tunics. You can identify the regiment by the number of buttons and the way they are spaced. From the chart below you can tell that the soldier on the right is a Coldstream Guard.

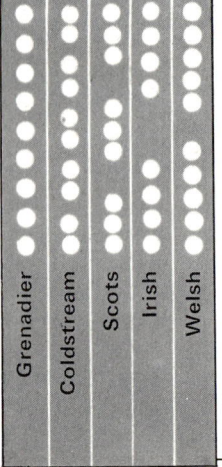

▲ With buttons and belt gleaming, a guard stands outside his sentry box dressed in a traditional uniform. The only odd note is the modern semi-automatic rifle he is carrying.

◀ A favourite time to visit Buckingham Palace is 11 a.m. This is the time for the Changing of the Guard. The guards who have been on duty that morning march away. Their place is taken by a new group of guardsmen who march into the Palace forecourt with a band. But during the ceremony there is often a large crowd of visitors at the railings and it can be very hard to see anything.

costume is kept just for ceremonies.

A Huge Home

The Palace is much bigger than it looks from the front as much of it is out of sight. The queen has her private rooms on the north side; facing the Palace, the north side is on your right.

Famous people are sometimes invited to a ball or banquet in the Palace. At the back of the Palace there are large gardens and a lake. Every summer hundreds of people are invited to parties here.

▲ The Palace and its gardens are private. You will see a long high wall to keep out unwelcome visitors. But there are two places where you can go in to visit. Both have their entrance in Buckingham Palace Road. The Queen's Gallery has some of the finest paintings from her private collection, and in the Royal Mews you can see the splendid royal coaches.

The Tower

The Tower of London lies close to the Thames at the eastern edge of the City. It has high towers and massive walls up to 4.5 metres thick at the base. In the past it was often used as a prison, but when the Tower was first built it was meant to keep people out, not in – it was a fortress!

In the 1070s the new king of England, William the Conqueror, was worried that his subjects were disloyal. He was afraid that Londoners might attack him, so he began to build a great castle with high walls to impress them with his power and make them too frightened to rebel. Although the fortress was not finished until after his death, it was so well made that it is still standing today, 900 years later.

The building is called the White Tower, and takes its name from the time of King Henry III who, in 1240, had the walls whitewashed inside and out. The White Tower is the oldest part of the Tower of London. It is almost square and has a small tower at each corner.

Later in that century, King Edward I had some new walls built around the White Tower.

Because the walls of the Tower are so strong it is a safe place to keep valuables, and our monarchs have kept the Crown Jewels here for centuries. Among them are crowns, sceptres and a golden ball called the coronation orb.

Nowadays the Crown Jewels are well guarded behind specially strong glass, but in 1671 they were almost stolen. A man named Colonel Blood came, disguised as a clergyman, to see the jewel-keeper. At first

▲ At the Tower you will see men dressed to look like soldiers from the 1500s. These are the Yeomen Warders, but almost everyone calls them Beefeaters. Every night the chief Yeoman Warder comes to the gates of the Tower. Soldiers guard him while he locks the gates with his keys. Hundreds of years ago, prisoners at the Tower could walk about inside the walls during the day. At night they were shut in their rooms and the outer gates locked. Nowadays there are no more prisoners, but the ancient ceremony still goes on.

he seemed friendly, then suddenly he and his cronies attacked the keeper. They hid one crown under the Colonel's cloak, another thief hid the orb in his trousers, but the gang was caught as it tried to get away and the treasures were saved.

The Bloody Tower
Along one wall of the Tower of London, on the side nearest the river, look for a building called the Bloody Tower. It takes its name from the murder of two royal children here in 1483. One of them, named Edward, would have been King Edward V had he lived. To this day, no one knows for sure who gave the order to do away with the two children.

▼ From high in an aeroplane, you can make out the plan of the Tower walls and the moat (which is now a well-tended lawn). Spanning the river in front is Tower Bridge.

Westminster

Kings and queens lived at the Palace of Westminster until the 1500s. There they met their advisers who helped them rule the country. These meetings became known as 'Parliament', a word that means a place for talking. Nowadays, kings and queens no longer live in the area, although Parliament still meets at Westminster. This is why the Houses of Parliament are sometimes called the Palace of Westminster.

In the Houses of Parliament, the laws of the United Kingdom are made. The elected MPs make speeches and answer questions, often disagreeing. Sometimes they shout and the meetings become very noisy.

In 1834, there was a great fire at Westminster which destroyed most of the old buildings. The Houses of Parliament we see today were built to replace them between 1840 and 1888.

The House of Commons
Inside Parliament there are two large chambers. One is known as the House of Commons, and this is for MPs (Members of Parliament) who represent the people. The other chamber is called the House of Lords. Everyone who sits in this chamber has to be a Lord or Lady, or a Bishop. Nowadays, the House of Commons is more important than the House of Lords, but any new law must be passed by both houses.

If you go into the public gallery of the House of Commons, you will see long rows of seats. They are called 'benches', but they are very comfortable and are covered with green leather. The MPs who support the Prime Minister sit on the benches on one side

▲ The name 'Big Ben' was originally used only for this famous clock's bell. But now people call the whole tower 'Big Ben'. The name comes from a large Welshman, Benjamin Hall, who was once in charge of the clock.

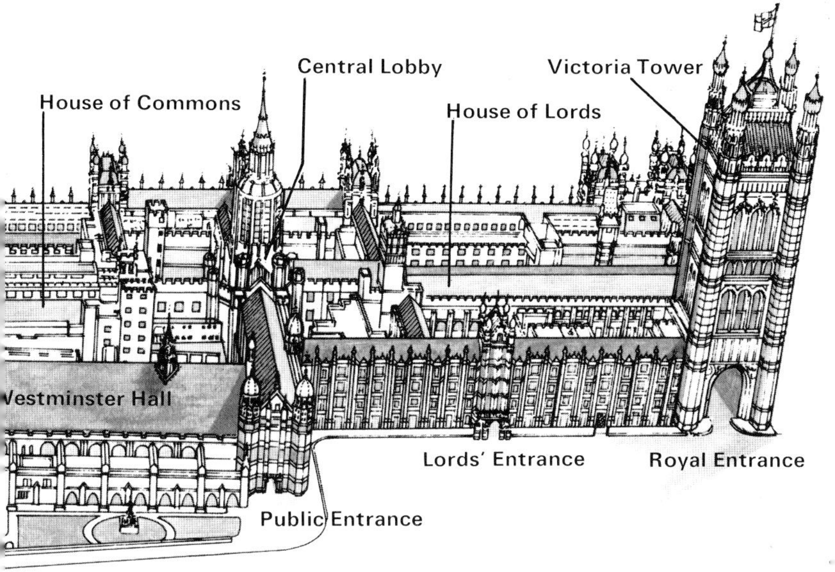

Labels on illustration:
- House of Commons
- Central Lobby
- Victoria Tower
- House of Lords
- Westminster Hall
- Lords' Entrance
- Royal Entrance
- Public Entrance

The House of Commons
1. Government benches
2. Opposition benches
3. Speaker's chair
4. Press gallery

of the chamber. The Opposition MPs sit facing them on the other side. MPs on one side are not allowed to walk across to the other side, just in case they start to fight. Hundreds of years ago, MPs sometimes fought each other with swords, and today the benches are still arranged in a way that prevents sword-fighting.

The Speaker

Between the Opposition and the supporters of the Prime Minister there is a table before which is a great throne-like chair. In this chair, wearing an old-fashioned wig, sits an MP called the Speaker. If MPs get too noisy, the Speaker calls out 'Order!' to make them quiet again.

You can visit the House of Commons and watch from the public gallery. The best way to get in is by writing to your MP who will send you tickets and arrange a tour. Take care to plan your visit for a time when Parliament is at work, as MPs have long holidays, especially in the summer.

Horse Guards

Close to the Mall, at the opposite end from Buckingham Palace, is Horse Guards Parade. Each year, on her official birthday in June, the Queen rides here on horseback to inspect her troops. The soldiers dress up in glittering old-fashioned uniforms and march to and fro around a large flag. This ceremony is called 'Trooping the Colour'.

Thousands of people come to see the ceremony. They write for tickets months in advance. The occasion is also broadcast on television. If the weather is hot, soldiers may faint and fall, but they are not allowed to move until the parade is over.

Every morning at Horse Guards Parade, mounted soldiers in ceremonial uniforms come to change places with the horsemen who have been guarding the buildings during the night. These are the Household Cavalry. They take their name from the fact that they once were the personal bodyguards of the royal household.

The building where the horsemen stand on guard is called the Horse Guards. It was built in the 1700s, and it used to be the headquarters of the entire British Army.

When Britain was fighting Russia during the Crimean War in the 1850s, it was at Horse Guards that the war plans were made. The officials here were known for taking a long while to make up their mind about anything. Florence Nightingale was a tough and clever lady who was shocked by the lack of medical care for soldiers. She became furious with army leaders, and wrote to them complaining that they couldn't even decide what to feed the Horse Guards' cat. Should it be given milk? Should it feed itself with

▲ King George IV was very tubby. So he was not very pleased when the Spanish sent him this short fat gun, called a 'bomb',

as a gift. In those days bomb was pronounced 'bum'. People soon began joking about George and his big 'bomb'.

mice? The cat might starve to death before they could decide.

The Turkish Cannon
On each side of the arched entrance way to Horse Guards Parade is an old cannon. To the right is a short, fat gun from Spain; left is a long-barrelled Turkish gun.

Another cannon that once stood near here was part of a plot to kill the King of England. In 1802, Colonel Despard and some henchmen set out to murder George III because they felt that the country did not need a king. They planned to fire the cannon at him as he rode past, but loyal Government spies learned of the plot in good time and Despard was arrested and put to death.

Beneath Horse Guards Parade is a network of underground rooms. Here the then Prime Minister, Winston Churchill, often worked in secret during World War II. You can go on a conducted visit if you want to see this underground bunker.

Other Palaces

Until the 1830s, when Queen Victoria moved there, Buckingham Palace was not the main royal home. Before then, kings and queens lived in St James's Palace. It's a smaller and more homely place than Buckingham Palace and you can walk right up to most of the Palace buildings.

The oldest parts of St James's were built by Henry VIII in the 1530s. A strong gatehouse was put up to defend the King, and although its old gates are battered now they still look very solid.

The grandest part of St James's Palace is called Clarence House. This big white building, near to Ambassadors Court, is the home of the Queen's mother. When she is there, her flag flies from the roof.

A Single Sentry
By the old gatehouse are two sentry boxes. A single guardsman stands duty here. As he marches up and down his boots ring out loudly on the stone; over the years sentries have worn out a great hollow in the pavement. The guardsman carries a rifle, although this is mainly for show. Usually it's not loaded as police are nearby in case of danger.

There is a famous balcony in St James's in a yard called Friary Court. The balcony runs along the far end of the courtyard which is usually deserted. It was the custom for crowds to pack into the courtyard on the day after a ruler died. Then the new king or queen would come onto the balcony and the crowd would give a great cheer of welcome. When King William IV died in 1837, the new Queen, Victoria, was brought onto the

▼ On duty at the gates of St James's Palace, a uniformed guardsman shelters from the rain in his sentry box.

balcony. She was only a girl of 17 at the time and when the crowd cheered, she did not know what to do. She turned to her mother for help and burst into tears – probably the first and last time a monarch has cried in public!

▶ This coin of Queen Victoria as a young monarch shows how she looked soon after she came to the throne of England.

A 'bun' penny

Hampton Court
When they began Hampton Court (above) it was meant to be the largest palace in Europe. It stood far outside London in the countryside. People travelled there by boat along the Thames and you can still do this today.

King Henry VIII lived at Hampton Court, at various times, with five of his six wives. But the Palace was originally built for someone else – Cardinal Wolsey.

Outdoors at Hampton Court is a famous maze. It is very easy to become lost among its tall hedges and it will take you a good few minutes to puzzle your way to the centre and back out again.

3: Waterways

London owes its life to the River Thames. When the Romans first came to settle in Britain in AD 43, there was no town where London is now. But the Romans needed a bridge across the Thames so that their soldiers could reach the Midlands and the east of Britain from the south. They built one at the first place where it was easy to span the river, close to the site where London Bridge is today. Traders as well as soldiers came to this spot to cross the river. Other people then made their homes around the bridge so they could sell things to the travellers who crossed here. The cluster of homes quickly grew into a little town. The Romans called it *Londinium* from which we get the modern word 'London'.

▶ There are about 30 bridges in Greater London. With the city's rapid expansion in the late 1800s many new ones were needed, and older bridges had to be replaced to deal with the increased traffic. The dates refer to the most recent versions.

Chelsea Bridge 1937

Albert Bridge 1873

Battersea Bridge 1890

▲ Every year crews from Oxford and Cambridge Universities race each other from Putney to Mortlake, a distance of 6.8 km. The race began in 1829 at Henley, but moved to Putney in 1845.

▼ Putney Bridge 1886

Wandsworth Bridge 1940

London Bridge

The previous London Bridge, completed in 1831 by John Rennie, was sold to America in 1971. It was removed stone by stone and rebuilt in Arizona.

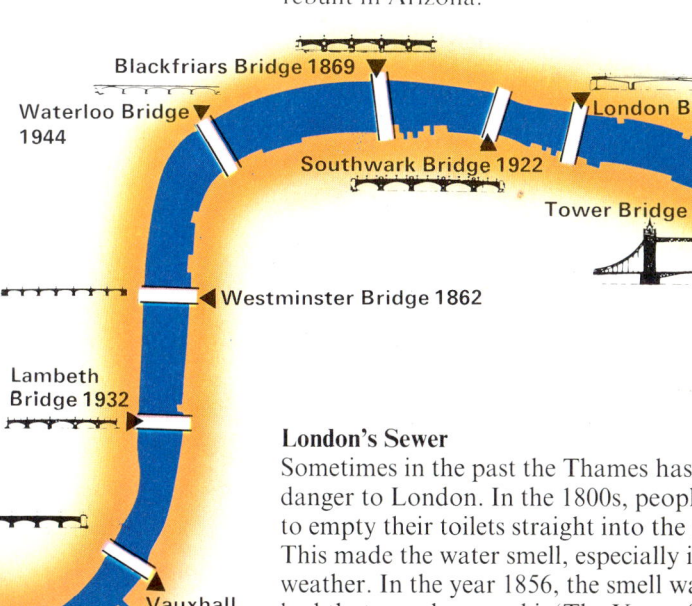

London's Sewer

Sometimes in the past the Thames has been a danger to London. In the 1800s, people used to empty their toilets straight into the river. This made the water smell, especially in hot weather. In the year 1856, the smell was so bad that people named it 'The Year of the Big Stink'. The filthy water also carried diseases such as typhoid and cholera. Thousands of people died, even the very rich. In 1861, Prince Albert, the husband of Queen Victoria, died of typhoid.

▶ The Thames Barrier can be found at Woolwich. It now protects London from the danger of flooding. This massive project was completed in 1984. When there is a threat of a very high tide the huge gates, each weighing 3700 tonnes, are raised to form a wall of steel.

Exploring the River

Along the banks of the Thames are many places to explore and to watch the river traffic. Here you can see slow barges with heavy cargoes and fast police launches. You can also learn how people in earlier times used the river.

At Richmond, to the west of London, you can watch the Thames flooding at high tide. There is a high, hump-backed bridge across the river at Richmond which was built in the 1700s. Nearby is a narrow street called Water Lane. It runs straight into the river and is used for launching boats. At high tide, the river covers much of the lane. One building here, called the White Cross Hotel, is sometimes cut off by the rising water. People in the hotel have to stay until the tide goes out again.

In the centre of London, near Villiers Street, there is a pathway parallel to the Thames called Watergate Walk. But nowadays you will not find any water here. The river, has gone, pushed back in the 1860s when the Embankment was built. What was once a shoreline of river mud at low tide is now a park – Victoria Embankment Gardens.

▼ The very large stone gateway in Victoria Embankment Gardens, decorated with anchors and seashells, is called a 'watergate'. This watergate was built around 1620, and was part of a palace owned by the Duke of Buckingham – at that time the richest man in England. Buckingham's guests used to visit him by boat, landing just outside the gate, which led through to beautiful gardens.

Elephant Tusks

Farther down the Thames you can walk between the Tower of London and the river. Along the path stand many old cannon. After you have gone under Tower Bridge you come to St Katherine Dock. This dock was built in the 1820s, and the tall warehouses standing next to it once stored exotic cargoes brought by sea from all over the world – spices, marble, perfume and ivory. It is because of the dock's connection with the ivory trade that you'll find statues of elephants on the gates at the main entrance.

A Yacht Harbour

Nowadays, there is a collection of historic ships in St Katherine Dock. The collection includes a lightship – a floating lighthouse – a fireship and *HMS Discovery*. This is Captain Scott's famous ship, built for him in 1900, for his first Antarctic expedition. Apart from old ships, barges and coasters, there are many private yachts berthed in the marina. You can cross a footbridge over part of the dock, and from this vantage point see the massive lock gates which are opened to let boats in and out when the tide in the river is high.

▲ At many places along the river people can walk on the muddy shore at low tide. Often they take metal detectors, trying to find precious things, such as coins, lost hundreds of years ago. In the 1800s, many boys and girls made a living by hunting along the river shore. They looked for bits of metal and rope which they could sell. These children were called 'mudlarks'. The work was dirty and cold. But they were poor, and collecting things from the mud was one of the few ways they could stay alive.

A Trip on the River

From a boat on the Thames you can see some of London's most interesting places. Westminster Pier next to the Houses of Parliament is a good place to start, because here you can catch a boat which goes to the Tower of London.

The first bridge the boat goes under is a railway bridge. When you have gone past, look back. You will see a special footbridge next to it called the Hungerford Bridge.

The shore on your left is man-made. Until the 1860s the river was much wider here. When the tide went out a wide, evil-smelling, muddy beach appeared. To make the shore higher, a strong wall was built and the space behind it filled with earth to create a strip of land known as the Embankment.

City Skyline

Next comes Waterloo Bridge. Just past it, look left to the skyline of the City. In the distance you may spot a church steeple which looks as if it was built in tiers like a wedding cake. It is part of St Bride's Church, Fleet Street. The church was built by Christopher Wren who wanted each of the many churches he designed to have a different shape. To the right you can see another of his buildings, the great dome of St Paul's Cathedral.

The next bridge is Blackfriars. After it, on the right, there is a big power station. The area where it stands is called Bankside. In the 1600s, this area was famous for its theatres and cruel sports. People came here to watch bull and bear-baiting, where the animals were tied to a post and fierce dogs were set loose to attack them.

▲ At the side of the Embankment stands a tall stone column with a pointed top. Its name is Cleopatra's Needle. It was made in Egypt about 3500 years ago. It is much older than the famous queen, Cleopatra of Egypt, who lived only 2000 years ago. But when people think of Egypt, they often think of her. So everyone calls it by her name. The bottom of the column is rather battered. In World War I, German planes bombed London several times. They didn't do much damage, but they did hit Cleopatra's Needle.

Next comes Southwark Bridge. Past it on the left are the two pointed towers of Cannon Street Station. There was once an arched roof between the towers that covered the railway tracks, it was taken down in the late 1950s, but because people liked the towers they were left in place.

The next bridge is London Bridge. The Romans built the first bridge across the Thames near here.

Over the centuries there have been many London Bridges. In the 1200s, a magnificent stone bridge was built to replace the wooden one that was in danger of collapsing. Houses were built along the sides of the new bridge, and for many years there were gruesome exhibits at each end. The severed heads of those who had been executed were stuck on poles and left there, rotting, as a warning to others.

The Trip Continues

After the boat has gone under London Bridge, you will see the Monument to the Great Fire of 1666 on the left. Nearby, toward the river, is the old Billingsgate Market building with its fish-shaped weather vanes. The fish market moved away in 1983, and the building is now being refurbished. Some kind of wharf has existed on this site for a very long time – possibly as far back as Saxon times.

This part of the river is called the Pool of London. Once ocean-going ships docked here. Tower Bridge had to lift its two great arms (called bascules) to let ships through. Nowadays, few ships come here and you'll be very lucky to see the arms lifting.

Tower Bridge was opened in 1894. Between the tops of

▼ Tower Bridge is built of steel. Its framework is cleverly hidden by a cladding of stone so that it looks similar to the medieval Tower of London behind it.

1) 1200-tonne bascules
2) Counterweight
3) Toothed track
4) Roadway
5) Control cabin
6) Engine
7) Steel-girder frame
8) Stone cladding

◀ *HMS Belfast* is a famous British cruiser of World War II.

its towers a metal walkway was built and pedestrians could cross it when the road bridge below was lifted. The walkway was closed for many years because too many people tried to commit suicide by jumping off it, but it is now open again.

Just before Tower Bridge, on the right, is moored a great grey warship – *HMS Belfast*. In 1943, in the icy waters off northern Norway, the *Belfast* helped to sink the famous German battleship, the *Scharnhorst*. Nowadays, the *Belfast* is open to the public.

Tower Bridge is the last bridge across the Thames. From now on the river gets much wider and instead of bridges there are tunnels. If you would like to go downstream, a boat will take you from Tower Pier to Greenwich.

Canals

In the years before 1830, there were no long-distance railways in Britain, and most roads were very rough. The easiest way to move heavy cargoes was by water, so dozens of canals were cut through countryside and cities. Today, there are still some interesting ones in London.

Early canal boats were pulled by horse. The horse walked beside the canal and towed the boat with a rope. You probably will not see any horse-drawn barges today, but beside every canal there is still the path, which the horses once used, called a towpath. You can walk along these paths in London for many kilometres.

The Regent's Canal, in north London, is especially pretty. You can get on to the towpath at Camden Lock (near Camden Town) or at Little Venice (near Warwick Avenue Station). Better still, take a ride on a canal boat.

One of the nicest ways to travel is on a canal boat called the *Jenny Wren* which leaves from Camden Lock. The boat is over 21 metres long but only two metres wide. Canal boats with this shape are called 'narrow boats'.

The *Jenny Wren* goes through a lock at Camden. Close to the lock an old footbridge crosses the canal. This was used to take the barge-horses from one side of the canal to the other. Farther along, the boat and towpath go through London Zoo.

Then come another two bridges. In 1874, there was a terrific explosion on a gunpowder barge at the second bridge. It killed the three men on board and blew up the old

▲ The British Waterways Board runs a waterbus along the Regent's Canal in north London. It goes from Little Venice to the zoo in Regent's Park.

▼ Canal boats are long and thin so that they fit into narrow locks. Early ones were horse-drawn and carried loads that were too heavy for the roads. Later ones had engines.

bridge. The bridge has been rebuilt, but it's still called 'Blow Up Bridge'. The first tree on the right, straight after the bridge, has a long crack down its trunk. This was made by the explosion.

Canal Locks
Canals are different to rivers. They do not flow downhill towards the sea. Instead, canal water stands still. If a canal is built on sloping ground it needs strong wooden gates, called lock gates, to hold back the water. Without these gates, the water would all run to the bottom of the slope leaving the higher parts dry.

When a canal boat wants to travel up a slope, it must stop in locks where the water level is adjusted to match the level on the other side.

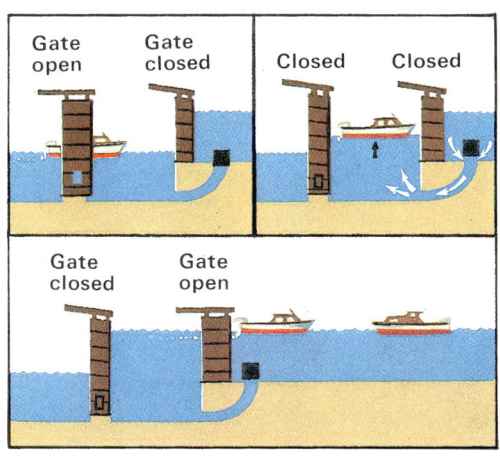

◀ Once a boat is in the lock, the gate is closed behind it. Then someone turns a handle to let water into the lock. Soon the water rises to the same level as that outside the second gate. Then the gate is opened and the boat goes through. The opposite takes place when a boat goes downhill. The locks are narrow so they fill or empty quickly.

4: The City

In Roman times, nearly 2000 years ago, London was a very small town on the north bank of the Thames, in the district where St Paul's Cathedral now stands. About AD 200, the Romans built a strong wall around the town to keep out enemies. Parts of this wall are still standing.

Nowadays, this old district is only a tiny part of London, but it is still called 'the City'. Another name for it is the 'Square Mile' because it's that small (about 260 hectares). The City has its own Lord Mayor, and own police force.

Some of London's most important businesses are in the City. At Smithfield meat market, the biggest in the country, you can watch porters heaving carcasses onto barrows and lorries – if you go early.

▲ City police have helmets with a high narrow crest on top that are different from other London police. City police do not patrol in the rest of London.

▼ The City is a very small part of London. You could walk from end to end in less than an hour. This map shows some of the main landmarks.

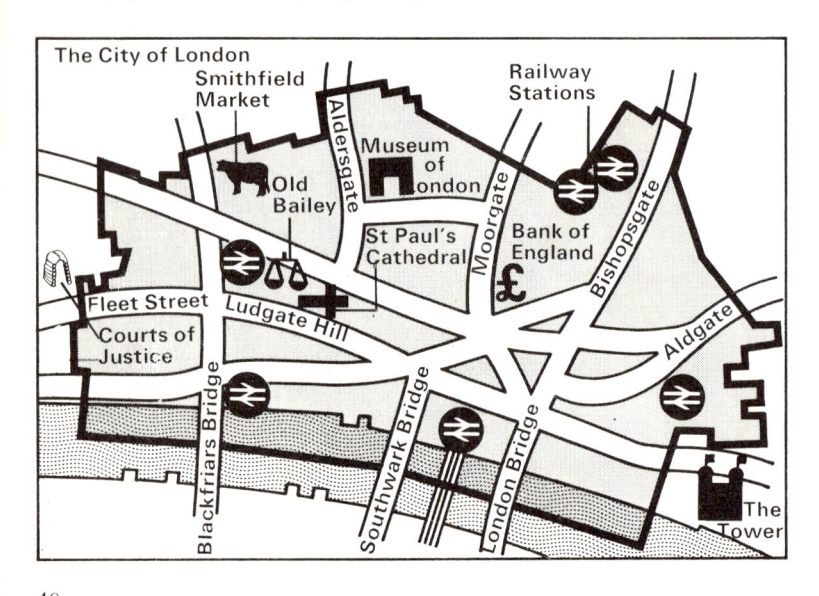

Most of the business of the City is to borrow and lend money. People's savings from all over the world find their way here via banks and insurance companies. You can see the offices of strange-sounding companies from the Middle East, America and Asia, among others, lining the streets. In turn, businesses and governments come to the City to borrow this money and use it to invest in things. They pay interest for the privilege and in this way City people make a living – and the owners of the money make a profit.

Long ago, in the years around 1200, strong gates were built into the old Roman wall. Today these have gone, although the street names tell you where the gates were – Aldgate, Bishopsgate, Moorgate and Aldersgate.

Until 1986 the Stock Market in the City was one of the most amazing and chaotic sights to see. Millions of pounds passed through a system that involved men in suits waving their hands at one another. After the 'Big Bang', when overnight the City started using computers, the Stock Exchange floor was abandoned as business moved to special dealing rooms where traders work from video screens.

▶ Every year a leading person in the City is chosen to be the Lord Mayor. Much of his job is ceremonial and each November he holds a big parade called the Lord Mayor's Show, when he rides through the streets in a fine horse-drawn coach. There are also bands, floats and people in costumes.

The City at Work

At night the City is almost empty. Hardly anyone lives here and the streets are so quiet you can hear the great bell of St Paul's Cathedral.

In the morning people arrive by the thousands. Some come on a special underground line from Waterloo Station, nicknamed the 'Drain' because of the way it 'flushes' people into the City!

▲ In the morning the roads and bridges leading into the City are solid with cars and people going to work. In the evening the traffic changes direction and takes them back home to the suburbs.

Bank of England
The busiest part of the City is by the Bank of England. The Bank lends money to all the other banks in the country. Huge stocks of gold are kept in its vaults and to prevent its theft, very few people are allowed in. If you go to the Bank you will notice that its walls have no windows near the street, to prevent thieves breaking in.

Next to the Bank is a tall building with pillars at the front called the Royal Exchange. High on its roof you will just be able to see a giant gold-coloured grasshopper which acts as a weather-vane. The first Royal Exchange was built here in the 1500s by a man called Thomas Gresham. The grasshopper was his symbol. The building burned down in the Great Fire of 1666, but Gresham is still commemorated by the grasshopper on the roof.

▶ Gatekeepers of the Bank of England wear peculiar uniforms. They are cut in an old-fashioned style to remind people of the Bank's long history.

▶ Not far from the Bank is Leadenhall Market. It has tall iron pillars inside decorated with dragons. People working in the City come here to buy meat and fish although some of the meat is unusual and therefore expensive. Grouse, birds from the moors of Scotland and northern England, are sold here and so are quail, birds small enough to be eaten on toast. In spring, seagulls' eggs are on sale too. They have green shells and are considered a delicacy by some people.

Legal London

One of the most fascinating places in the City is the Old Bailey, the courts where people are put on trial for the most serious crimes. Each court has a special gallery set aside for the public, but you must be at least 14 years old to go inside and watch a trial in progress.

Accused people sit in a wooden-walled box about four metres long called 'the dock'. In the old days docks had spikes along the top to stop the accused escaping. Nowadays, a warder sits in every dock as a guard. Below the courts are the holding cells where prisoners are kept until they go back to gaol.

The judge sits behind a high table and wears a white wig. The barristers who stand before him also have wigs and long black gowns. They argue before the court about whether the accused are guilty or innocent of the crime with which they are charged. Near the judge sit 12 men and women called the jury. After hearing the arguments of the barristers they decide if the accused are guilty or not. If they say 'guilty', then the judge decides on a punishment. If they say 'not guilty', the people on trial are set free then and there.

Until 1902, people on trial at the Old Bailey came from Newgate Prison nearby. Newgate was old, dirty and stank terribly. When the prisoners came into court, the smells came with them, so before the courts went to work, scented herbs were brought in to hide the stink. Newgate Prison was knocked down eventually, but the court officials had grown fond of the herbs and, even today, herbs are still brought into court.

▲ Barristers have dressed in almost the same way for hundreds of years. They can be seen walking to and from the Royal Courts of Justice wearing their old-fashioned wigs and their long swirling black gowns. This is the 'uniform' they wear when they appear in court.

The Courts of Justice

A few metres outside the City, in the Strand, is another court building, the Royal Courts of Justice. It has turrets on its roof and tall pointed windows. You will not see many police or prisoners here as most of the cases tried in these courts have to do with commerce and business.

Near to the Law Courts is an area called the Temple with many old buildings and courtyards. Barristers have their offices here. Close to Temple Church, in Inner Temple Lane, is the tomb of a lawyer who died in 1726. His statue is on top of the tomb and it shows him wearing a long wig and two white strips of cloth, called bands, instead of a necktie. Barristers still wear bands today, 250 years later.

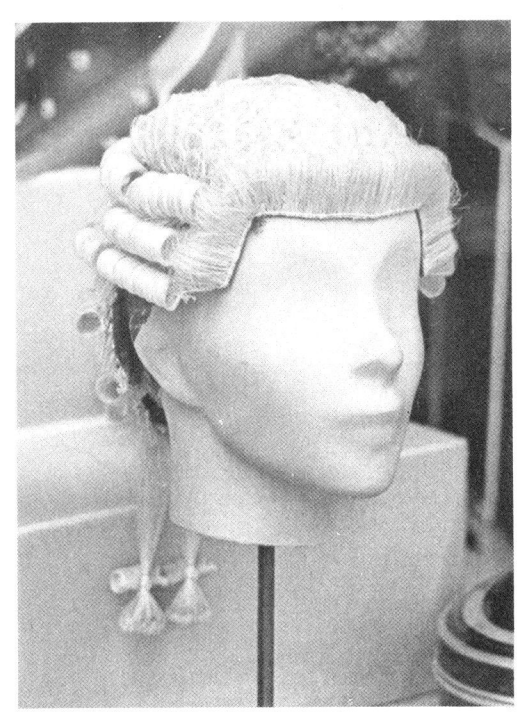

▶ Lawyers' wigs are made in a shop in Star Yard near to the Royal Courts of Justice – you can see one in the window. Women make the wigs, which have two little pigtails at the back, out of horsehair. Wigs like this one are expensive to make and cost lawyers a lot of money.

A Citywalk/1

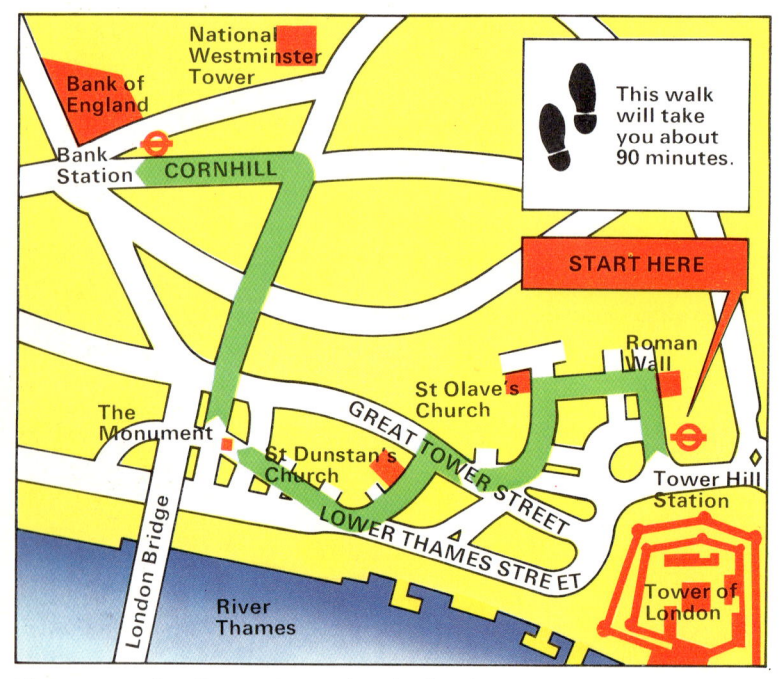

Map labels:
- Bank of England
- National Westminster Tower
- Bank Station
- CORNHILL
- START HERE
- Roman Wall
- St Olave's Church
- The Monument
- St Dunstan's Church
- GREAT TOWER STREET
- LOWER THAMES STREET
- Tower Hill Station
- London Bridge
- River Thames
- Tower of London

This walk will take you about 90 minutes.

If you go to the City at the weekend when it is quiet, you will find there are lots of interesting things to see. Start your walk at Tower Hill Tube station. When you come out, look to your left and you will see the Tower of London across the road. Near to you, on the path, there may be some men with tiny monkeys. They hand the monkeys to visitors then offer to take their photographs. But beware – being photographed with a monkey costs quite a lot.

Now turn right and leave the Tube station. About 100 metres along Cooper's Row there's an opening to the right under a building and often there is a fountain

▲ The map above is of the route of a walk through the City. The places you see here are described in the next few pages.

▶ This decorative panel of a rich man and his family shows that his three children all died when they were young. The father married three times, and his wives are shown too. Around all their necks are large frilly collars called ruffs, worn around 1600.

playing. Behind it is a high stone wall from which the ground at the front has been cut away to show what was originally built by the Romans. You are now standing just inside the old Roman city. The Romans built the wall in layers with tiles. A wall built in this way is immensely strong.

Step back a few metres and you can see the top of the wall. It was built in about AD 1200, 800 years after the Romans left. Near the top there are openings in the stone, like windows, which were made for archers to shoot arrows through. About a metre from the top is a level walkway where guards used to stand on watch. Halfway up the wall is a line of holes that once held wooden beams for a roof or platform. Nowadays pigeons sit here, sheltering from the rain.

Now leave by the way you came, cross the road and walk along Pepys Street to St Olave's Church. Above its iron gate you will see skulls. The man who had them made was a stern Christian. He wanted to remind people that they would die one day and to make them think about heaven. Go into the church and turn right. High up on the wall at the end is a pretty plaster panel of a rich man and his family in old-fashioned clothes. The Latin writing underneath tells people all about them.

▲ A very famous man is buried in St Olave's. His name was Samuel Pepys. He wrote an extemely rude diary in the 1660s. When he was in church, Pepys used to stare at pretty ladies through a telescope and when women sat near him he sometimes tried to grab them. This made one lady so cross that she tried to stick a pin in him to make him stop!

A Citywalk/2

After coming out of the church gate, go right into Seething Lane; this leads you to Byward Street. Keep right into Great Tower Street and go as far as a narrow lane called St Dunstan's Hill where you'll find a ruined church – St Dunstan's-in-the-East. It was bombed in World War II, and has never been repaired.

The churchyard is now a pretty garden, with kestrels nesting high in the church's steeple. Kestrels are a kind of hawk and it's very unusual for them to live in a city. They are here, however, because there are so many pigeons for them to prey on.

Farther down St Dunstan's Hill is a main road called Lower Thames Street. Across it to the right is where Billingsgate fish market used to be. The market has now moved to new premises on the Isle of Dogs.

The Great Fire
Just past the old market is a very high pillar called the 'Monument'. It was put up in the 1670s to commemorate the Great Fire of London which raged for five days and burned down most of the City. The fire started in a little street close by called Pudding Lane. On top of the Monument is a spiked golden ball which stands for the flames.

The Monument was designed by Christopher Wren, the man who built St Paul's Cathedral. Wren was also an astronomer and at first he wanted the Monument to be a great telescope. He hoped to put powerful lenses at the top so that astronomers could stand at the bottom and see the stars magnified, but the pillar was not built high enough for this.

At the bottom of the Monument, on the far side, is the stone figure of King Charles II. He was King when the fire raged and he helped rebuild London afterwards. On his head, Charles has a long wig. From the mid-17th century, kings and their courtiers often wore spectacular, decorative wigs. That's why, even today, powerful people are sometimes called 'big wigs'.

◀ Tradition says that if the Monument to the Great Fire of 1666 was laid on its side, it would reach the site of the bakery where the fire broke out.

Look up Fish Hill, away from the Monument, to one of the tallest buildings in Britain, the Nat West Tower. Just before it, turn left into Cornhill. A little way along is an old water pump that's painted blue and gold. It was put there in the 1700s when most people did not have water in their homes.

A little farther down Cornhill is the Bank of England and the Tube at Bank Station.

▲ Looming high above the rest of the City is the 183-metre National Westminster Bank Building. Sometimes kestrels circle about it, soaring high on the strong updrafts that the building creates.

5: Sinister London

In the 1600s and 1700s murder and robbery were very common in London. Sometimes the robbers worked on horseback, and were called highwaymen. They stopped carriages and threatened to shoot any passengers who didn't hand over their money and jewels.

The Dancing Highwayman
Claude Duval was a famous highwayman in the 1660s. He stopped a coach one day and found a young lady inside. Before stealing her money, he asked to dance with her. Then he let her go and, to thank her for the dance, only took a quarter of her money!

Until the 1800s, the punishment for robbery was often death. When Claude Duval was caught he was executed by being hanged in public at Tyburn, a favourite place for executions. The site of Tyburn is now called Marble Arch. In the past, huge crowds came to see hangings here and the condemned were brought through London on carts from Newgate Prison. On their way, they were sometimes given beer to drink by people who felt sorry for them.

When the time came to die, the criminals stood in the cart with a rope around their neck. The other end of the rope was tied to a wooden frame called the gallows. Then the cart was driven away and the criminal was left hanging. This was a slow and very painful death which relatives and friends tried to make quicker by pulling at the legs of the hanged person to end their suffering.

Before they were hanged condemned people were allowed to make a speech. Even

▲ In the 1600s and 1700s, highwaymen attacked coaches in lonely stretches of the countryside to rob rich passengers.

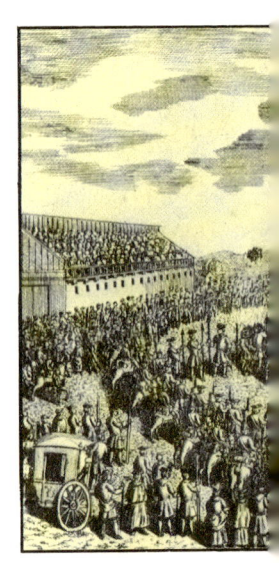

Colonel Despard, the man who tried to kill King George III, was allowed to make a speech to the crowd before his execution. When he spoke, the rope was already round his neck. If he had tried to say anything against the King, he would have been hanged immediately before he could finish.

Public Hangings

In the 1800s, public hangings also took place outside Newgate Prison in a street called Old Bailey. Eight o'clock on Monday morning was the time for executions and people got up early to see the hangings on their way to work. Some wanted a really good view of the criminals as they died, so they paid money to watch from the windows of the houses opposite.

Even small crimes were punished with death. In the 1800s a postman was hanged for stealing one letter. But one criminal, a man called Whitehead, was sentenced to hang for a theft and was able to cheat the gallows. He had often worked on high buildings and was very good at climbing, so one day before the date of his execution, when he was in the prison yard at Newgate, he waited until the guards were out of sight then began to climb the high wall at the corner of the yard. He went up by pressing his back against one side and propping his feet against the other wall. When he got to the top he was spotted by a woman who lived outside the prison, but she felt sorry for him and didn't raise the alarm, and so he escaped.

The Last Hanging

Public executions were stopped in 1868, partly because the crowds had been behaving very badly, shouting at the condemned people. The last hangings that took place in Britain, in the 1960s, were all for murder.

▼ This public execution at Tyburn is of a lord who murdered his steward, and was hung in 1760.

Child Thieves

In the 1800s many of London's thieves were children. They lived dangerous and uncomfortable lives in the streets, where they stole purses and expensive silk handkerchieves. At night they climbed into houses to burgle them, and when they were caught, the children were sometimes given horrible punishments.

Some children had parents who didn't want them. Children like this often ran away, but they found it hard to get enough money to live. The law allowed them to work in factories, but the work was dangerous and the wages low. Many children took to stealing instead.

▲ Children who were trained pickpockets would run through London's crowded streets, snatching gold watches and helping themselves to the silver snuff boxes and coins in people's bags and pockets.

Thiefmasters
Men called thiefmasters controlled these children, making them hand over the things

BOYS EXERCISING AT TOTHILL FIELDS PRIS

they had stolen so the children never even benefitted from the risks they took.

Thiefmasters gave lessons in picking pockets to their child thieves. One used to hang a coat on a line with its pockets full of handkerchieves. Then he told the children to go up to it and gently take them out. Any child who made the coat swing on the line was not being careful enough and would be knocked down and kicked and made to try again. Other thiefmasters used to sew little bells on to coats. A small mistake would make the bells ring.

One group of child thieves lived in an old van near the Thames. They stole from the crowds of people who used the river boats. Their thiefmaster was a man called Larry and if children did not obey him, he didn't let them sleep in the warm van. You can still see one of the places where these children used to go. It is a little yard in the area called the 'Adelphi' just by the Strand. You will find it beyond a small gate in Robert Street.

▲ Thiefmasters taught children to break into houses. A child would climb in through a very small window that was not locked, and then open the door. The grown-up burglars would walk in and rob the house. This is why even tiny windows were often barred.

Policemen sometimes did not want to arrest children caught stealing. A big policeman looked like a bully if he dragged a child of eight or nine along the street. The children knew this and used the trick of lying down in the street and crying, hoping the policeman would feel ashamed and let them go.

Many child thieves were unlucky and were sent to prison, sometimes to be hanged. In 1830, a nine-year-old boy was sentenced to death for breaking a window and stealing some ink, while another was deported to Australia. This was his punishment for stealing a saucer and a guinea pig.

Some children had better luck though. One boy of 12 stole so much money that he owned his own home and had a girlfriend to live with him.

A Grim Death

Nowadays Lincoln's Inn Fields is a pretty park in the middle of London. People play tennis under the trees, or drink tea and have picnics. But this was once a grim place – during the day it was used for executions and at night it was full of thieves.

At the centre of the Fields is a ring of tall trees. Start your walk inside this ring, where you'll find a small wooden shelter. Look at the middle of its floor and you will see a metal plaque which says that near here, in 1683, Lord William Russell was beheaded. King Charles II and his brother James thought that Russell had planned to kill them. Russell was actually innocent, but Charles and James refused to believe the evidence that proved this.

Afterwards, Russell's friends took his head and body into a house at the edge of the Fields, where they sewed them together so he could be buried in one piece.

Hung, Drawn and Quartered

Earlier, in 1586, some plotters were executed in these Fields. They had tried to kill Queen Elizabeth I because they wanted her cousin, Mary Queen of Scots, to rule instead. When they were caught they were sentenced to be hung, drawn and quartered. They were hung for a few seconds, but they were not dead when they were cut open and their insides were pulled out. This was called 'drawing'. Then each man was hacked into four pieces – or 'quartered'. Afterwards their heads were cut off and the executioner boiled them, so they would not decay too quickly, and put them on show.

Walk out of the Fields, until you see an old house with tall windows across the road. Number 59–60 Lincoln's Inn Fields was built in 1640. Here William Russell's body was sewn together.

Outside the house are battered iron railings and three tall poles. These were made in the 1700s to hold oil lamps and keep thieves away. At the top of each pole is a loop which held a globe of glass with an oil lamp inside. Every evening a lamplighter came along with a ladder to fill the lamp and light it. You can still see the bar, near the top of each pole, where the lamplighter rested his ladder.

The thieves who waited in the Fields across the road mainly robbed people in very dark places because in well-lit areas the victims could see who was robbing them, and afterwards the thieves might be recognized.

In this house, around 1800, lived a man named Spencer Perceval. You can see a plaque with his name to the right of the door. In 1812, when Perceval was Prime Minister, a man called Bellingham, who thought the government had cheated him, walked up to Perceval in Parliament, pulled out a pistol and shot him dead.

▲ This old drawing shows the only Prime Minister ever to be shot in Britain.

◀ Around the corner from Lincoln's Inn Fields, in Portsmouth Street, is 'The Old Curiosity Shop', a name made famous by a Charles Dickens novel. Supposedly it's the same shop, except that Dickens said 'the old place had long ago been pulled down'.

Beheaded!

When William the Conqueror built the Tower of London, he wanted his new fortress to make people fear and respect him. Later monarchs also used it to make their enemies afraid of them, sometimes imprisoning people there for years and years. But only people from rich or famous families were executed in the Tower; other prisoners were killed outside the walls, where the crowds could watch.

Queen Anne Boleyn, the second wife of Henry VIII, was beheaded in the Tower in 1536. Henry had wanted her to have a son, but her only living child was a girl, so Henry decided to cut off Anne's head and to marry another woman instead.

Anne was terrified of dying, and asked Henry for a sword to be used, not an axe. Before the execution she tried to cheer up, telling herself that her neck was small enough for the sword to cut through quickly.

Another unlucky Queen was Jane Grey. She was a brave and clever girl, but she had unpleasant parents. Her father forced her to marry a man she didn't want to because she was descended from Henry VII. After Edward VI's death Jane was proclaimed Queen of England, but she was Queen for only nine days. Her rival Mary Tudor, Edward's sister, defeated her. Jane was locked in the Tower and sentenced to death. She was only 16.

At her execution she was blindfolded. But with the blindfold on, Jane could not find the block where she was to place her neck. For a time no one would help her. Then finally she was taken to it and the executioner cut off her head.

▼ Queen Anne Boleyn being executed in the Tower of London.

▶ The axe and chopping block that were used to behead people at the Tower are still on display there. Victims knelt at the back of the block, putting their neck on the flat surface, and their face in the hollow part. Then the executioner chopped off their head with the axe.

A Royal Prisoner

One famous prisoner in the Tower went on to become the ruler of England. Princess Elizabeth was taken there by boat in 1554, on the orders of her half-sister, Queen Mary. When she went in from the river through the Traitors' Gate, she was very frightened and started crying, but she was let out soon afterwards. When Mary died, the Princess became Queen Elizabeth I.

The Tower has strong walls and in the past was always well guarded. Even so some prisoners have escaped. One man climbed down the walls on a rope which some friends had sent him in a barrel of wine. Another prisoner had a visit from his wife and a woman servant. Just before the time of execution, he swapped clothes with the servant, then walked out of the prison dressed as a woman. The guards did not notice and he escaped to Italy.

The last prisoner to be beheaded in England was Lord Lovat, in 1747. He had plotted against King George II and was executed outside the Tower. You can find the place, in the little park outside Tower Hill Tube station, where a sign still marks the spot.

6: A Rainy Day

One of the best places in London for spending a rainy day is the Science Museum near South Kensington Station. There are many famous tools and machines here. Some of them are from the early 1800s when steam-powered machines were new, while others are from the space age.

In the past, steam-driven machines were used to do many kinds of work once it was discovered that steam, let out through a system of valves and pistons, was powerful enough to pull entire trains.

▶ One steam engine in the Science Museum was made in 1813. It is one of the earliest models and was called 'Puffing Billy', because of the way it chugged along blowing out steam. It trundled along at about 8 km/h pulling coal trucks. Displayed nearby is a rare motorbike built in 1889. Today, motorbikes are all driven by petrol, but the museum's model was powered by steam. It has a small boiler which hangs between the two wheels.

▶ The launch position of an astronaut can be seen through the door of the original Apollo 10 capsule.

In the museum you can hear a recording of the first man-made sound from space, the 'bleeping' of the Russian Sputnik I, launched in 1957. Close by is the American Apollo 10 which went around the Moon in 1969. Also on show are the astronauts' food and clothing, including the special 'nappies' they wore under their spacesuits.

On the top floor are the old Hurricane and Spitfire war planes of World War II. These fighters look old-fashioned now, though they were once among the finest planes in the world. In 1940, they fought in the 'Battle of Britain' against invading German bombers and fighters.

In the basement, you can look into a submarine periscope and watch people on the floor above. There are pulleys to tug that show how easy it is to lift heavy weights, machines to test whether you are colour blind, and a safe which you can try to 'burgle'. An invisible ray guards it – if you walk through an alarm buzzer goes off.

59

Monsters and Mummies

Not far from the Science Museum is the Natural History Museum. Just inside the doors are skeletons of huge dinosaurs. There are no dinosaurs alive today – they all died out millions of years ago – but we know about them because their bones were fossilized and have since been dug up. In the museum you can also see the fossils of plants, fish and other strange creatures that died millions of years ago.

In another part of the museum are rows and rows of owls. Their round, flat faces look quite friendly, but their beaks and claws are hooked for tearing prey.

One of the biggest, the snowy owl, is about 60 centimetres long. It has a white face and body which serves as camouflage because it lives in the Arctic where there is snow nearly all year long. The animals it hunts have trouble seeing it against the snowy background until it is too late. Nearby is a tiny owl no bigger than a sparrow – the pygmy owl.

▼ The Natural History Museum has many displays of dinosaurs. You can see giants such as Tyrannosaurus, a 15-metre flesh-eater, and the horned Triceratops, a fierce-looking vegetarian. The small Ornithomimus was an ostrich-like creature.

Tyrannosaurus

Triceratops

Ornithomimus

The British Museum

This museum is in the centre of London. In it you will find paintings made by the Egyptians and Ancient Greeks over 2000 years ago. The Egyptian ones are in the same gallery as the famous mummies. These were once the bodies of rich people that were chemically treated so they would be preserved.

The Ancient Greek paintings are on pottery. One painting, in Room 3, shows a man and woman fighting each other with spears. The man is winning, and you can see the blood spurting from the woman's neck.

▼ This picture of a farmer ploughing and seeding his fields comes from a beautiful piece of pottery made in Ancient Greece. There are many pots like this in the Museum which show scenes from everyday life.

Other paintings show women beating men.

In Room 9 of the museum are pictures of Greek women dancing and playing the harp. The pictures are tiny – sometimes less than two centimetres high. They are engraved on precious stones. When a Greek sent a letter it was often sealed with a blob of wax, stamped by one of these stones. People who received the letter then knew who had sent it.

If you are a stamp collector, go into the King's Gallery of the British Museum. There is a long wooden case with dozens of drawers; in each are rare and precious stamps. The famous triangulars, used in the 1800s in Cape Colony, South Africa, are especially beautiful.

▲ This fragment of parchment is from an Egyptian painting. It shows a warrior hurling a special throwing-stick to hunt marsh birds.

Pictures That Tell a Story

In the National Portrait Gallery, near Trafalgar Square, there are paintings of well-known people and famous events in British history. Most of the paintings were done before photography was invented, and they are our only way of knowing how famous people looked. Many also tell interesting stories about events in the past.

In Room 19 of the gallery, there are pictures of the Crimean War of the 1850s. The Crimea is in southern Russia. British and French troops were sent there to help the Turks against the Russians. During the war British horsemen made a disastrous attack called the Charge of the Light Brigade. The horsemen rode straight towards the Russian cannons, and were slaughtered. There is a picture of this famous event, showing rows of cavalry charging into battle. Some horses and riders are already down, shot by the Russian cannons.

The person who did the most to look after wounded soldiers in the Crimea was Florence Nightingale. You can see a picture of her, standing in her wartime hospital at Scutari (right). The hospital was in a dreadful state before she arrived. It stank of dirt and disease, and the floor crawled with insects. Even the drinking water for the wounded men was germ-ridden. More were dying of disease than on the battlefield. By her intelligence and courage, Florence Nightingale changed the hospital into a clean, properly run place, and brought professional nursing to the battlefield. She is regarded as a founder of modern nursing.

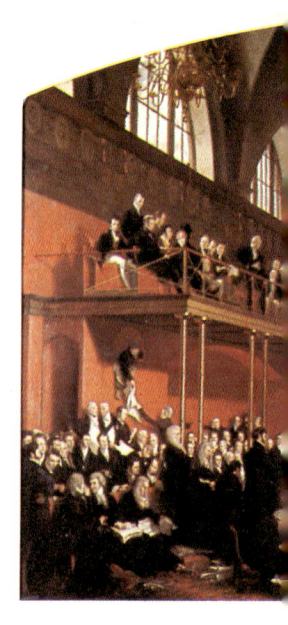

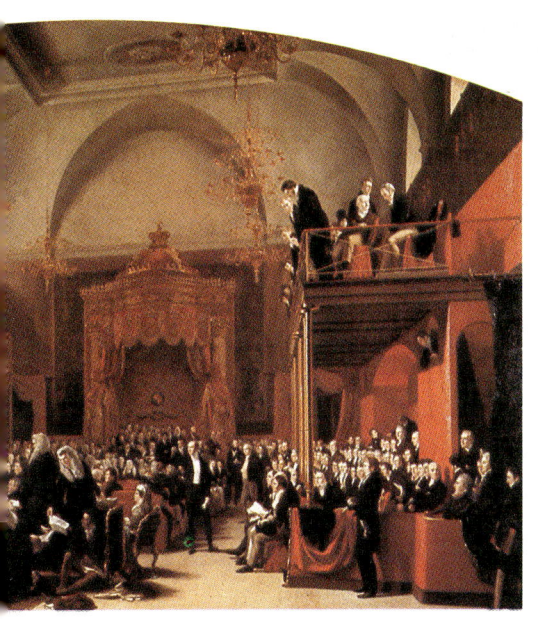

◀ Look in Room 15 for the picture of a famous trial – that of Queen Caroline, wife of George IV. The king and queen were not very fond of each other. He had lots of girlfriends and she had many boyfriends. In 1820, George tried to divorce her, his lawyers accusing her of being unfaithful. The huge painting shows the Queen listening to the trial in the House of Lords. Her lawyer, who is wearing a long white wig, is standing up to defend her. Her enemies, all friends of George, are looking down at her from a gallery. They include George's brother William (who had ten children without ever bothering to get married). Queen Caroline forced George to stop the trial, but he never allowed her to act as his Queen. When she tried to take part in his coronation, in 1821, George told his soldiers to keep her out. Soon after this disgrace Queen Caroline died.

Little Museums

Pollock's Toy Museum is located in an old house with twisting staircases and tiny rooms. Its old toys are fascinating for people of all ages, and show how people dressed and made their homes in the 1800s and early 1900s.

There are dolls from the 1800s made of wax with long dresses and lace collars. Some of the dolls were made for boys, like 'Action Man' today. Boys' dolls from World War I show how British sailors and soldiers dressed at the time. Sailors had white uniforms and soldiers flat, peaked caps. There are also models of early tanks and biplanes that were used in that war.

On one wall there are comics from the early 1900s. Old copies of *The Beano* and *Dandy* are there, as is an even older comic called *The Magnet*. The cover announces that it is 'Billy Bunter's own paper'; the first stories about him were written in this comic.

▲ This tiny museum is crammed with toys, games and miniature figures. There are also many kinds of toy theatres to see. If you walk upstairs, be sure to look around at the detailed dolls' houses.

Inside the houses are models of old-fashioned lights, cupboards and chairs.

◄ One house is called 'Struck by Lightning'. Outside the house on a balcony, is a doll dressed in a servant's uniform of about 1910 – black dress, white apron and white cap. She has just been cleaning the windows with a mop, but she seems to be falling backwards from the balcony, as if lightning has hit her and knocked her down.

The Museum of London
This museum, near Barbican Station, has many objects on show that are thousands of years old. Near the entrance is a collection of flint hand-axes from the Stone Age, about 200,000 years ago, used to kill and chop up animals. You can see how the axes were sharpened by being chipped along the edges. One axe was found near Piccadilly, now one of the busiest streets in the world. But when the axe was made, the area was open countryside. A few people, dressed in skins, stalked wild animals here for food.

Many thousands of years later, just before the Romans arrived, Ancient Britons lived where London is now. These people were called Celts. Their fine metal swords and helmets can now be seen in the Museum.

▼ The most exciting model in the London Museum is of the Great Fire of 1666. While you're looking at it, you can hear the story of how the fire spread, as written by Samuel Pepys, who actually helped to fight the blaze. The model seems to burst into flames as the fire spreads. The old cathedral of St Paul's lights up too. At the end of the display, you will get a surprise reminder of how hot the fire was.

Crowns and Crosses

111 metres high

Entire dome weighs 65,00 tonnes

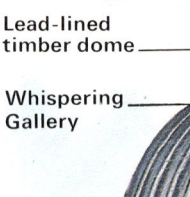

Lead-lined timber dome

Whispering Gallery

Almost everyone who visits London hopes to see St Paul's Cathedral and Westminster Abbey. In the summer, these buildings get very crowded so it's easiest to visit them at other times of the year.

St Paul's is one of the most famous buildings in the world. The whole cathedral took 35 years to build, from 1675 to 1710, and Christopher Wren was the architect who designed it. Before he could build St Paul's he had to knock down the remains of the cathedral destroyed by the Great Fire. He tried using gunpowder, but an assistant's mistake caused a terrible explosion. People complained about the noise, so Wren had to knock down the rest of the building using a huge wooden battering ram to smash the old walls down.

If you go inside the cathedral look up at the dome. Far above, you will see two walkways (called galleries) running around the inside. The lower one is called the 'Whispering Gallery'. When someone in the gallery faces the wall and talks quietly, their voice can be heard clearly at the far side more than 30 metres away.

Near the main altar is the area called the choir. Above the choirboys' seats, the roof is decorated with glittering glass and stones of many colours. In the passage between the choir seats and the cathedral walls, there is an old stone statue showing a man with a beard and loose-fitting clothing. This is John Donne, a famous poet who died in 1631, and who thought a lot about dying and heaven. His statue shows him wearing a shroud – the clothing he was dressed in to be buried.

Cone-shaped brick dome carries 711-tonne lantern and cross

Eight stone pillars support the dome

Inner dome

Westminster Abbey

Westminster Abbey is older than St Paul's. Most of it was built in the 1200s and 1300s. From inside you can see that the roof is decorated with delicate lines of stone, looking rather like cobwebs. This decoration is called 'fan tracery'.

When kings and queens begin their reign, there is a special service in the Abbey. This is called the coronation, the ceremony at which the crown is put on the new monarch's head. The ceremonial crown is too heavy to be worn for long, so after a few moments it is replaced by a lighter one.

Just inside the main door of the Abbey is the Tomb of the Unknown Warrior. An unknown British fighting man from World War I is buried here in honour of the many soldiers killed in battle whose bodies could not be recognized.

Shop Windows

It is not easy to describe the tremendous variety of shops in London. You can find places that sell only harps or only model railways, while others carry nothing but cigarette cards, masks and costumes, fireworks or toys for children. Browsing past all the windows of shopping streets like Oxford Street and Kings Road would take days.

Hamley's in Regent Street (right) is one of the biggest toy shops in the world. On the floor that sells trains there is a huge model railway layout that runs around the shop. The locomotives make puffing and whistling sounds as they chug along.

Harrods, a department store in Knightsbridge, also has a very good toy department. Often there are puppet shows here, as well as many toys you can try out for yourself. The best time to visit Harrods is in the months leading up to Christmas when there are special displays.

There are many shops that cater for people with special hobbies. If you are looking for ballet equipment, for instance, Freed's in St Martin's Lane carries most of what you will ever need. In the Strand there is a famous shop for stamp collectors called Stanley Gibbons; their collection of catalogues will tell you about almost every stamp in the world. The stamps here are not bargains, but all are in good condition. The rare ones are worth hundreds of pounds.

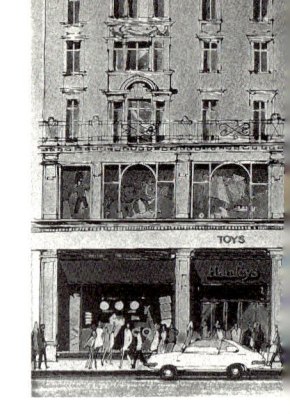

In Neal Street there is a shop that stocks dozens of different kites. They come in the shapes of birds, planes, insects, bats, sailing ships and dragons. Certain kites, which are controlled by two strings, are used to perform highspeed aerobatics. In London, kites are not supposed to be flown on lines longer than 60 metres in case they become a danger to low-flying aeroplanes. But sometimes people fly them as high as they can, until they are almost invisible from the ground. Some of the best places to see kites being flown are Parliament Hill, on Hampstead Heath, and Blackheath.

Davenport's is a shop specializing in magic and tricks. It used to be opposite the main entrance to the British Museum, but can now be found in the Charing Cross Underground Shopping Arcade. Inside, you can examine magicians' kits and learn how to perform dozens of stage tricks.

◀ Close to Charing Cross Station is a shop selling magic tricks and toys.

▲ A shop in Covent Garden, crammed with almost every sort of kite.

7: Outdoor London

▼ In the west of London, close to the Thames, is Kew Gardens, with its famous collection of rare plants, shrubs and trees set out in a huge park through which the public can wander. The Wood Museum at Kew is a good place to learn about the different types of trees in the world, while the tropical greenhouses are like miniature jungles. Inside one, in the steaming heat, are giant ferns and floating water lilies the size of mattresses.

London has more parks than almost any other city in the world. There are over 18,500 hectares of public green space. Almost all of this grassland and wood is open to the public. Some parks, like Hampstead Heath and Richmond Park, are so big that you can easily get lost in them.

The Heath is a hilly place of woods, lakes and hidden streams that extends over 300 hectares. Even at weekends, when many people go for a walk here, or fly kites and play sports, there is always plenty of room to escape the crowds. Near the north end of Hampstead Heath there are fairs on Bank Holiday weekends. On the side towards Highgate is a chain of small lakes. Some are open for swimming, others are used only for fishing. The lakes are fed by a spring that rises here. Once it flowed through London as the River Fleet, but now it is part of the storm sewer system. At the southern end of the Heath there is a sports ground and an adventure playground.

◀ At one end of Hyde Park, near Marble Arch, is Speakers' Corner. On Sundays people stand here and talk to the crowds about absolutely anything they like – except treason. Some speakers are very serious, some are just there for fun. Best of all – it's free!

Right in the middle of London is Hyde Park. It has a long, winding lake called the Serpentine where people come to swim, fish and go for boat rides. There is a path for riding horses through the park called Rotten Row. No one knows why it is called that, although some think the name came from the French *Route du Roi*, which means the King's Way.

Crystal Palace Park, in south London, has 20 dinosaurs among its trees and pools. The models are life-size and scattered about as if in the wild. They are not very accurate models, as you can see by the fact that their makers put *Iguanadon's* thumb on its nose!

London Wildlife

London is full of wildlife. Many animals and birds choose to live here because there is plenty of food and shelter in the city. Some are very bold – though they do not let people touch them, just in case someone tries to catch them. But others are shy and come out mainly at night.

Bird Life
Many thousands of sparrows live in the city. Most are shy, and nest high up on the sides of buildings, but a few tamed sparrows live in St James's Park near The Mall. At the bridge over the lake in the park there is a special place for feeding them; here the birds hover and snatch up breadcrumbs that are held out.

Thousands of pigeons are fed by people in Trafalgar Square. Little pots of seed are sold here and when someone holds out seed for the birds, the pigeons perch on their arms and shoulders to eat it. Pigeons live in railway stations too. Railway staff do not allow them to be fed here, however, as the birds make so much mess.

In Leicester Square, starlings roost in their thousands. If you look around the square on a dark winter evening, you may think that there are leaves still on the trees, but these 'leaves' are really flocks of starlings. At dusk they whistle to each other until the whole square seems to vibrate with their noise.

Many wild birds live near water. Some of the most unusual ones in London are best seen at large reservoirs, such as Barn Elms, on the edges of the city. Here, where serious birdwatchers go, binoculars are a great help.

If you walk along Regent's Canal in the

Pigeons

Rat

Mouse

Starling

Mute swan

spring, you will see ducks and ducklings gliding near the banks. You may also hear wrens singing in the bushes. A wren's song is fast, quavering and very loud; you wouldn't think it came from a bird with a body barely seven centimetres long.

▶ In some places you can see half-wild creatures in London, such as the herd of deer and the rabbits in Richmond Park. On Wimbledon Common and in Epping Forest, foxes and badgers make their burrows in dense thickets. During the day they stay hidden but at night they come out to hunt and feed.

Animals That Live Near People

Hundreds of thousands of rats live in London feeding on the rubbish left by humans. They steal food and can be found almost anywhere. One very expensive shop in Knightsbridge even has its own rat-catcher. He comes in the evening, when the customers have gone home, and uses a gun to stop rats raiding the food.

In London, mice have taken to living in the Tube system. At many stations you can see them scurrying about the rails feeding on chocolate wrappers, gum and cigarette ends, while the racket of the trains seems not to worry them at all. Mice also live in houses, in the spaces between ceilings and floors. They may grow very large and some even seem to thrive on the poison set out to kill them.

Zoo Life

London's biggest and most famous zoo, with more than 8000 animals, is in Regent's Park. This is one of the best places in the world to see large wild animals. The big cats, such as lions, tigers and leopards, are kept in roomy fortified enclosures. So are the rhinos, polar bears, giraffes and elephants – though you can often see the baby elephants out for a walk.

The Zoo has special times for cleaning and feeding the animals. The elephants have their bath in the morning, and in the afternoon the penguins are fed. Penguins are kept in open enclosures with pools of water where they can swim.

Some of the animals look cuddly, though if people tried to hug them they would probably bite. Pandas look friendly enough with their white faces and big black rings round their eyes, but they are shy and do not like to be touched. The Arctic fox looks like a furry pet, with a coat of white for camouflage in the snow. But foxes, too, will bite if someone frightens them.

The Wolf Wood is an odd place to visit. Here, a pack of wolves have a roomy enclosure planted with trees and bushes, just like their home in the wild. They trot back and forth along regular paths from one end to the other. The wolves look like Alsatian dogs, and if someone walked one on a lead, hardly anyone would notice it was not a pet.

People often ignore animals in the street. In the 1970s, one man used to take his pet lion cub for a walk through shopping centres in north London. Hardly anyone seemed to notice; perhaps people thought it was a Golden Labrador dog!

At the Regent's Park Zoo, a Giant Panda feeds on bamboo while an African elephant is given a cooling bath. In summer, you can even take camel rides.

Small Zoos

London Zoo has huge bills to pay for feeding and looking after its many animals and birds, so tickets cost quite a lot. But there are smaller zoos and farms in London which are cheaper or even free. In Clissold Park, in north London, you can see Chinese deer, cranes and peacocks. At the City Farm, on Grafton Road in Kentish Town, there are donkeys, pigs, sheep, ducks and other farm animals. Here, on an old railway site that has been turned into a piece of countryside, a farm has come to the city.

In south London, Crystal Palace Park has a children's zoo which is open in summer. There is a talking mynah bird here which is very popular and can say 'Who's a pretty boy?' so clearly that you can hear its London accent! There are also small travelling zoos which visit other parks in the summer.

Street Markets

Busy street markets are some of the best places for finding bargains, and also for watching people at work. The stallholders know that they must catch the attention of shoppers so that they'll look at their stall and not someone else's, and they make a great deal of noise as they tout their goods! Middlesex Street (which everyone calls Petticoat Lane) has dozens of stallholders like this on Sunday mornings.

One stallholder, who sold china in a London market, had a clever trick for making people buy. When he was short of customers, or when people were hesitating, he shouted that he was going to break some of his plates. People stopped and stared as he stacked the plates in his arms, throwing them into the air, and letting them break. He then threatened to break some more, unless people started to buy. Some shoppers, not liking to see waste, would rush to buy the remaining plates to rescue them from being broken. In this way, the stallholder lost a few plates, but made a profit by getting rid of all the rest.

Most street markets are open at the weekends, when people have plenty of time to shop. Different markets are famous for different kinds of goods. Petticoat Lane, the biggest street market in London, is like an outdoor department store and is especially well known for its clothes and linen. In Club Row, not far away, many sorts of small pets, such as fish, guinea pigs, birds and gerbils, are sold on Sunday mornings. Columbia Road market in Hackney has rows of flowers and plants on a Sunday morning, and in west London, Portobello Road

▲ A dealer of 'antiques' (and odd junk) rests by his cluttered stall in the Portobello Road market. Around him moves the busy Saturday morning crowd of shoppers.

market is at its busiest on Saturdays selling antiques as well as junk.

If you are interested in old and foreign coins, you will enjoy exploring the market in The Arches, at Charing Cross Station (the Arches is a passageway off Villiers Street).

At all the markets the stallholders keep a sharp eye for thieves. In the 1800s, Petticoat Lane was famous for its bold thieves, who even included some of the stallholders. It was said that people could have their handkerchief stolen when they entered the market, and by the time they were leaving someone would already be trying to sell it back to them.

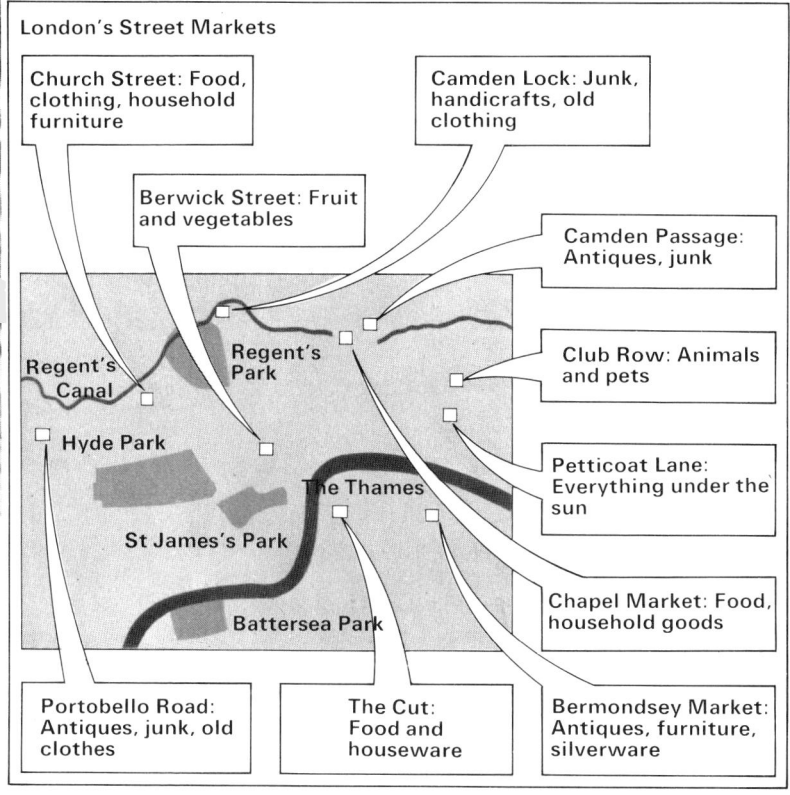

London's Street Markets

- Church Street: Food, clothing, household furniture
- Camden Lock: Junk, handicrafts, old clothing
- Berwick Street: Fruit and vegetables
- Camden Passage: Antiques, junk
- Club Row: Animals and pets
- Petticoat Lane: Everything under the sun
- Chapel Market: Food, household goods
- Portobello Road: Antiques, junk, old clothes
- The Cut: Food and houseware
- Bermondsey Market: Antiques, furniture, silverware

Secret Railway

You can have an exciting day out on the North London Link, a train route not many people know about. Highbury and Islington Station is a good place to get on. Look right at the next station, Caledonian Road & Barnsbury (1), and you will see a building with a very tall chimney which is Pentonville Prison (2). Rows of little square windows mark the prisoners' cells.

After the station look left, where soon you'll have an unusual view of central London. In the distance is a big red building with pointed towers which is St Pancras Station (3). Farther to the right is the tall column of the Telecom Tower (4).

After Camden Road (5) and Gospel Oak Stations, there is an adventure playground on the right (6) with fields behind it that are part of Hampstead Heath. Soon after, you

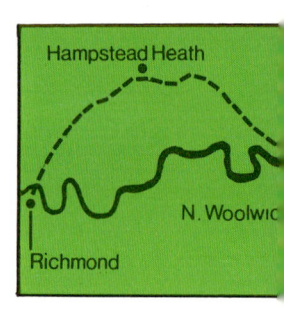

▲ The North London Link runs from North Woolwich – close to the Woolwich ferry – in a great arc through northern London. It meanders past endless rows of houses, skirts Hampstead Heath and crosses the Grand Union Canal twice. Finally it clatters over the Thames and stops at Richmond.

will see well-tended gardens beside the track that were once waste ground. Look out for two large white boxes about a metre high which are beehives. The bees get their nectar from the plants of Hampstead Heath, then store it as honey inside these hives.

Farther along the route is Willesden Junction Station (7) where you can see express trains going beneath you on their way from Euston Station north to Birmingham and Manchester. Soon after, the train crosses the Grand Union Canal (8).

After leaving Gunnersbury Station, the train crosses the Thames (9). Look out for the houseboats where people live on the river. If the tide is out you will see great stretches of mud bank at the river's edge. As you reach the far bank, look to the left and you will see a modern building on stilts called the Public Records Office (10). Valuable papers are kept here describing what happened in the past. The building was designed with stilts so that if the Thames flooded the papers wouldn't get wet.

Richmond
The train ends its journey at Richmond (11). Here you can get out and go down to the Thames and maybe go fishing (12). There was an old palace nearby, where Queen Elizabeth I died in 1603, but all that remains now is a blue plaque on the wall of the building that occupies this historic spot.

8: Things to Do

It is easy to watch Londoners going to and from work, but it is not so easy to see what they actually do there. If you want to find out what happens inside some of the skyscrapers, office buildings, factories and shops in London, the best thing is to go on a guided tour.

One of the biggest sorting offices in Britain is at Mount Pleasant not far from Kings Cross Station. Here, letters from all over the world arrive and are directed to their London destinations. Much of the sorting work is done by machine and you can go on a two-hour tour of Mount Pleasant and see it all for yourself.

Even more interesting is a tour of the King Edward Building in the City, where you can discover an underground railway owned and run by the Post Office. A miniature electric train runs under London from Paddington Station in the west all the way to Liverpool Street and Whitechapel in the east – over 10 km. It is loaded with mail sacks and runs automatically – there is no driver.

In Covent Garden there is a small, very smart-looking shop called Penhaligon's, where you can watch perfumes being made. The shop is open on weekdays, and if you are with an adult you can go in and watch through a glass screen as people carefully blend the scents. You may even be allowed to sniff a sample of the perfumes.

Right in the heart of the City there are stables where shire horses are kept. Shires are working horses and Whitbread Breweries still uses them today to haul wagon-loads of barrels around London delivering beer to pubs. Shires are gigantic beasts, weighing a tonne on average, and they're able to pull loads of up to four times their own weight.

Visitors can tramp around the sawdust-strewn floors of the stables and meet the horses, as well as watch the blacksmith at work at his furnace, or see the shires being fed one of their five huge meals as they munch their way through almost 27 kgs of chaff, fodder, carrots and horse nuts every day.

Ford of Dagenham, to the east of London, has free tours of its vast car-building works – which are about the same size as the whole of the City of London. Here, visitors can see cars being built from start to finish. On the assembly lines, around 1000 cars a day are put together. Thousands of workers and robots attach or check a part of each car as it glides past on a huge conveyor system. At the end of the line, finished cars are tested and driven away to an outdoor parking compound, then loaded onto transport vans or railway wagons to be delivered.

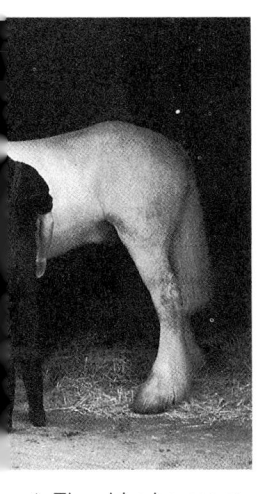

▲ The shire horses at the Whitbread Stables are used to deliver beer to pubs – the old way.

▼ New cars are checked as they leave the assembly line.

Addresses

For visits to the Post Office, write to The Controller, Mount Pleasant Sorting Office, EC1, or to The Controller, King Edward Building, EC1.

Penhaligon's perfume shop is at 41 Wellington Street, WC2.

To visit the shire horses write to the Whitbread Stables, Garrett Street, London, EC1.

Tours of the Ford Motor Company can be arranged through the factory Tours Office, Room 3/001, Ford Motor Company, Dagenham, Essex.

Sports to Watch

Even when you do not have much money, you can always find exciting sports events to watch in London. The choice is huge, and includes cricket, football, rugby, tennis, basketball, hockey, judo and riding, among many others.

▶ Cricket is a very complicated sport. The bowlers may take hours to defeat the opposition, and spectators are often happy whoever wins.

▶ London offers some of the best football in the world, with usually three or four First Division clubs and many in the lower Divisions to watch. At First Division matches, tens of thousands of supporters come out for Saturday afternoon games. It's a good idea to reach the ground an hour before the match so that you can stand in front and have a view that isn't blocked. At matches in other Divisions, crowds are often much smaller.

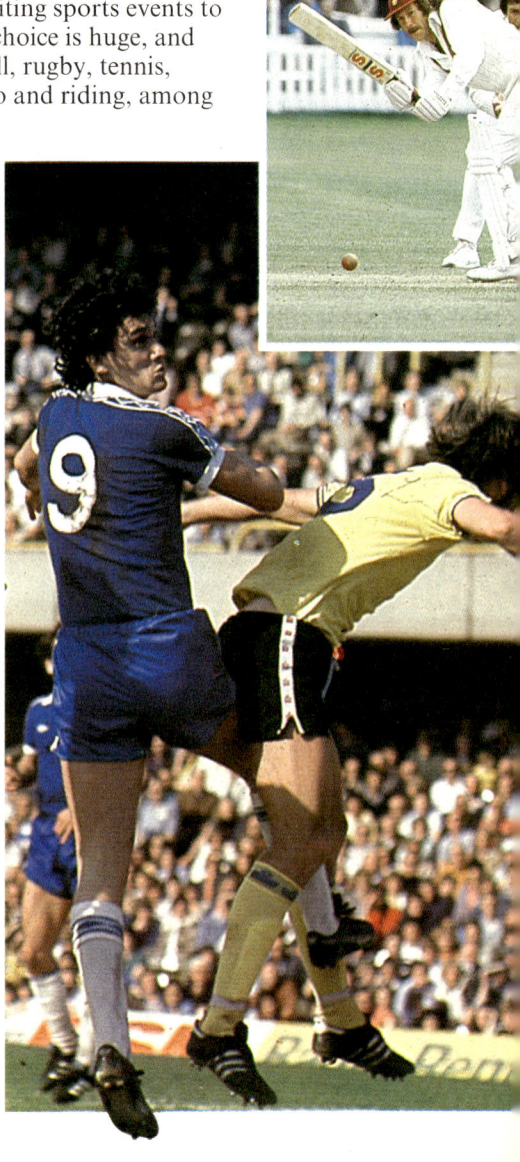

For tennis, the Wimbledon finals late in June are the high point of the year. Though the finals are expensive, you can often get cheap tickets for the early days of the competition to watch some of the world's best players.

Watching a cricket match is a lazy way to spend a summer day. Cricket is like fishing; for a long time not much seems to be happening, then suddenly something exciting occurs, usually just as you've taken your eye off the game! The best-known London clubs are Middlesex, at Lord's Cricket Ground, and Surrey, at The Oval.

▼ Wimbledon's grass courts are world famous. The greatest players come here every year in June for a fortnight of exciting tennis.

Athletics
Major international events are held at Crystal Palace Sports Centre.
Boxing
Important fights are staged at Wembley, Earls Court and the Royal Albert Hall. The newspaper *Boxing News* lists bouts.
Cycling
Six Day races are great to watch. Contact the British Cycling Federation for details of these races.
Rugby
Major Rugby Football matches are held at Twickenham. The Rugby Football Union gives details of the dates.
Show-jumping
The two main jumping shows of the year are in July and October at Wembley.

Sports to Try

Watching sports can be very exciting but the only way to find out what it's like to play is to take part yourself.

If you would like to organize your own game of football, cricket, or even baseball, it's usually easy to find a place to play in a public park. At some parks it's necessary to book a pitch beforehand by asking the park attendants to reserve one.

There's a huge variety of sports available in London and if you wish to sample some, the best place to go is a sports centre. There are more than ten of them in and around London. Each one offers dozens of different activities and they are all under cover so there is no reason for rain or cold to spoil your fun.

At Crystal Palace, in south London, more than 50 different sports are available on the various pitches, in the courts, the swimming pool and in the gymnasium. The Michael Sobell Centre, near Finsbury Park, offers even more. Here you can try your skill at trampolining, karate, boxing, fencing, dancing, badminton, and many other activities.

▲ Fishing is far more exciting than many people think and is one of the most popular sports in the country. Half the skill lies in finding the places where the fish are hiding; the rest lies in waiting patiently for the moment when your float is suddenly jerked under water and you feel a fish pull on the line.

Dozens of species of fish have been caught in London including tench, pike, roach, dace, perch, carp, bream and eels.

In most waters in the area you will need to have a Thames Waterways Board licence to fish. You can get one cheaply

Skiing

Although it seldom snows in London, this doesn't stop people from going skiing. At the Michael Sobell Sports Centre you can ski indoors on a machine between October and March. At Crystal Palace, and at Alexandra Palace in north London, there are artificial outdoor ski slopes and both experienced skiers and beginners come here to learn and to improve their skills. The slopes are open all the year and lessons are given in autumn and winter.

from a fishing tackle shop; it will allow you to try your luck in the Thames and the canals.

You'll need a different licence to fish in lakes and ponds in the parks, though some are free. Park attendants will tell you what to do.

It is said that the best fishing in London is in the reservoirs that have been specially stocked with trout. A daily ticket to fish here is not cheap, but it will let you take home up to half a dozen good-sized fish, if you can catch them. The best guide to London's many fishing sites is a book called *Where to Fish*.

Riding

Most people would not expect to find horses in central London though it is perfectly possible to go riding here. There are four stables close to Hyde Park where you can hire horses and ponies by the hour. You can take them into the Park for a ride on the sandy trail known as Rotten Row.

Unusual Activities

It's almost an impossible task to list all the things you can do in London. Here are a few activities that not many people know about, but which many would probably enjoy doing.

You probably know how to copy the design of a coin by putting a sheet of paper over it and rubbing with a pencil. In a similar way, but taking more care, you can make superb copies of the commemorative brass plaques of medieval knights and ladies that are found in churches.

If you pick one that's on the floor, you can cover it with a large sheet of paper and rub over it, lightly at first and then harder until you have a beautiful copy on your sheet. A good place to do brass rubbing is at All Hallows-by-the-Tower near the Tower of London, and at the Brass Rubbing Centre in St James's Church, Piccadilly. If you have not tried it before the staff will show you what to do.

There is a charge for making the rubbing which also includes the materials you'll need. Ask for one of the small figures when you first start as they are cheaper than big ones.

▲ At night, the green dome of the London Planetarium becomes the setting for a spectacular laser light and music show.

Roman Detective

If you go hunting for signs of London's past you will quickly learn things that few Londoners ever know about. For example, there are still Roman remains that you can explore, and the Museum of London produces a map of them.

Near to the Museum of London are the ruins of a Roman fort. In the museum itself is a pot which has the word *Londini* on it. This is the oldest surviving example (from before AD 100) of the city's name. There is also a stone model of the god Mithras killing a bull, and in Queen Victoria Street are the foundations of a temple to him.

At the entrance to the church of St Magnus-the-Martyr, in Lower Thames Street, you can see an ancient wooden post, which is thought to have belonged to the wooden bridge that the Romans built here – the original London Bridge!

▲ For a time, the god Mithras was as widely worshipped in Roman Britain as was Christ.

London is not a very good place to study the sky. The haze from street lights hides most of the stars. But you can find out a lot about them at the Planetarium near Baker Street Station.

The London Planetarium has a superb 35-minute show of the Milky Way and the Solar System that describes how planets, moons, comets and stars move through the heavens.

At the Greenwich Royal Observatory, which was once used by Sir Isaac Newton, there are diagrams of the stars and the sky that can be seen from London with the help of a telescope. Next door, at Flamsteed House (left), is the red time ball, which drops down a mast each day at exactly 1 p.m., Greenwich Mean Time. In the Meridian Building there is a collection of old telescopes, and on the floor of the building a metal line marks the meridian. On maps this point is called zero degrees longitude.

9: In a Year

The events in this list take place every year, though the exact dates may vary. To find out exactly when and where they occur, ring Kidsline (222 8070) or the Visitors and Convention Bureau (730 3488).

JANUARY
Chinese New Year This takes place at a slightly later date than the European New Year, and happens late in January or early February. The Chinese people of London stage a big street festival in Soho where the highlight is the Lion Dance by young men dressed in a lion costume.

FEBRUARY
Cruft's Dog Show Early in the month, the best efforts of British dog breeders can be seen at Cruft's, held at Olympia Exhibition Hall.
Clowns' Service This church service for clowns is at the Holy Trinity Church in Dalston. Afterwards, the clowns, many in costume, give a free show.

MARCH
Oxford and Cambridge Boat Race The race, for crews of eight rowers, is a traditional contest between the universities of Oxford and Cambridge. The crews race along the Thames from Putney to Mortlake, and crowds watch along the way. If you're lucky, you may see a crew sink and have to be rescued.

EASTER

Easter Parade In Battersea Park on Easter Sunday there is a colourful fair all day and a parade with bands, floats and sideshows.

Harness Horse Parade On Easter Morning, a show and judging of work horses and their colourful carts and vans takes place in the Inner Circle of Regent's Park.

APRIL

Tyburn Walk This procession, on the last Sunday of the month, starts at the Old Bailey and follows the route by which victims were taken to the Tyburn gallows. The Walk is to remember Catholics who were hanged at Tyburn for their beliefs.

MAY

Cup Final The high point of the English football season is the match played at Wembley Stadium on the second Saturday of the month. Close to 100,000 people go to the game.

London Private Fire Brigades Competition London has more than 60 private fire brigades. Each year they hold a contest to see which is the most accurate at hitting fires. The contest is in Guildhall Yard; you'll need waterproof clothing to watch.

JUNE

Trooping the Colour This magnificent ceremony to celebrate the Queen's official birthday is held at Horse Guards Parade. You will need tickets to watch, which are hard to obtain. You'll have to write to the Brigade Major, Household Division, Horse Guards, Whitehall. The ceremony itself is held on the Saturday nearest to June 11th. The rehearsal two Saturdays before is free.

Wimbledon Tennis Championships For two weeks at the end of the month, the world's best players meet here on the grass courts.

▲ Harness Horse Parade.
◄ Cruft's Dog Show.
▼ Oxford and Cambridge Boat race.

JULY

Doggett's Coat and Badge Race The race for single oarsmen was first rowed in 1714. It's along the Thames from London Bridge to Chelsea and the winner is given a silver badge and orange coat to wear.

Royal International Horse Show This world-class horse-jumping competition is held in mid-July at the Empire Pool, Wembley. Royalty usually come to the show.

Swan Upping In the third week of July, six boats leave Sunbury-on-Thames, west of London, and head for Whitchurch, with their crews dressed in old-fashioned clothes. On the way, they catch and count the swans on the river and nick the beaks of the young swans, or cygnets, to show who owns them.

AUGUST

Notting Hill Carnival A noisy and colourful West Indian celebration turns the streets around Portobello Road and Notting Hill into a two-day festival at the end of the month.

Late Summer Bank Holiday On Sunday and Monday, great fairs are held on Hampstead Heath, Blackheath, and Wormwood Scrubs.

SEPTEMBER

Battle of Britain Week Fighter planes fly past Westminster Palace and over London to remind people of the RAF's narrow victory over the German Luftwaffe in 1940. The ceremony is on the nearest Sunday to September 15th, just before noon.

Last Night of the Proms In mid-September, the last night of the season's Promenade Concerts is traditionally a wild occasion when the audience, wearing odd costumes, sings with the orchestra and waves banners and signs. Tickets are by ballot only and are highly prized.

▲ A rider clears a high-hurdle at the Royal International Horse Show.

▲ A group of Pearly Kings gather together outside St Martin-in-the-Fields at Trafalgar Square.

◀ A costumed dancer parades through the streets during the Notting Hill Carnival.

OCTOBER

Pearly Harvest Festival On the first Sunday of October, at the church of St Martin-in-the-Fields in Trafalgar Square, the Pearly Kings and Queens gather for a colourful service. They are Londoners who wear clothes covered with pearl buttons and are best known for the charity work they do.

Lion Sermon This odd sermon is preached in St Catherine Creechurch in the City for a 19th-century Lord Mayor who narrowly escaped from a lion in Arabia.

Opening of the Law Courts Soon after October 1st, judges and barristers walk in robes and long wigs from Westminster Abbey to the House of Lords after a special service. This is followed by a procession at the Royal Courts of Justice in the Strand.

NOVEMBER

London to Brighton Vintage Car Run On the first Sunday in November there's a race of vintage cars from London to Brighton. The race is very slow and stately by modern standards, and the cars set no records except for endurance-without-breakdown. The run starts from Hyde Park Corner.

Lord Mayor's Show On the second Saturday of November, the newly-elected Lord Mayor of the City rides in his carriage from Guildhall to the Law Courts in the Strand. The procession, which began in the 1200s, is accompanied by a great parade.

DECEMBER

Cat Championship Show The National Cat Club holds its yearly championship at Olympia; a great chance to see rare cats.

Street Decorations for Christmas From the start of the month, Regent Street and parts of Oxford Street are lit up by a mass of bright lights and decorations.

10: Places to Visit

Tours & Visits

The advantage of being a visitor to London, rather than a native, is that you get to see lots more of the wonderful things the city has to offer than any born-and-bred Londoner, who means to but never has the time. Remember, it's useful to phone first to check opening hours and prices, as these things seem to change every season.

Airports

If engine noise is music to your ears then you'll love Heathrow Airport, where during peak times a plane a minute touches down. At the Spectators' Roof Garden you'll be able to watch aircraft loading and unloading on the parking aprons next to the terminal, while in the distance you'll see two runways being used at the same time – one for takeoffs and the other for landings; it's a plane spotter's idea of heaven.

At Gatwick Airport there is a Spectators' Gallery on the roof of the Arrivals Hall where you can watch the same kind of scene.

British Airports Authority, Queen's Building, Heathrow Airport, Hounslow, Middlesex TW6 1JH. Tel: 01-745 7224. Open daily from 10am to dusk. Admission £0.20. Gatwick Airport, Gatwick, West Sussex RH6 0NP. Tel: 01-668 4211. Open daily 9am–4pm. Admission £0.15.

Cabaret Mechanical Theatre

Automata are mechanical figures, usually of people or animals, that seem to move of their own accord but are actually powered by clockwork mechanisms. The main

TOURS & VISITS

difference between robots and automata is that the latter are usually doll-like figures dressed up to look like real people and animals. A fantastic amount of detail is put into them to fool you into thinking they're alive. Their arms and legs move about, hands pick up and hold things, mouths open, close and seem to eat and drink, and heads turn and eyes blink.

This tiny museum houses a small but amazing collection of automata, hand built by as inspired a lot of artists and inventors as you'll ever come across.

Cabaret Mechanical Theatre, Unit 33, Covent Garden Market, London WC2. Tel: 01-379 7961. Open daily 10am–7.30pm summer, 12 noon–6.30pm winter. Admission £1.00 adults, £0.50 children.

Changing of the Guard

One of the great royal traditions in this country takes place every day outside Buckingham Palace and Horse Guards Parade – and it's free! You don't have to be a tourist to go along – though you'll be forgiven for thinking that it helps. In mid-summer it often looks like half the world and his mother have travelled to England just to see this ceremony.

The soldiers and cavalry who stand guard during the night are replaced each morning, in a big and noisy ceremony, with a new lot. You can choose to join the huge crowd at the railings of Buckingham Palace or else go down to the Mall to Horse Guards Parade where there is more room to watch. Or, if you want to see the guards with almost no one else around you can look at them forming up in the courtyard of Wellington Barracks in Birdcage Walk (a short distance away from the Palace), or see the Household Cavalry mount their magnificent black horses in front of Hyde Park Barracks.

Changing of the Guard, Buckingham Palace, The Mall, London SW1. Daily from 11.30am. Admission free. Changing of the Guard, Horse Guards Parade, Whitehall, London SW1. Mon–Sat from 11am, Sun from 10am. Admission free.

TOURS & VISITS

Cutty Sark & Gipsy Moth IV

In her heyday, in the 1870s and 1880s, the *Cutty Sark* was the fastest tea clipper in the world. She was a huge ship, kitted out with 16 kilometres of rope and 3000 square metres of sail. In 1871, she set a record of 107 days for bringing a cargo from China to Britain via Cape Horn. Getting the new season's tea crop to market first was a fiercely contested race in those days.

Today you can visit the ship where she lies at Greenwich, and walk around her decks and holds. In case you wondered, her name comes from Scottish slang and means either a mischievous or teasing woman in a short dress, or a stubby clay pipe – we think it's the former, given sailors' preferences about these things.

Next door is the tiny *Gipsy Moth IV* in which Sir Francis Chichester sailed single-handed around the world in 1967 – a sea-faring first.

Cutty Sark, King William Walk, Greenwich Pier, London SE10. Tel: 01-858 3445. Open Mon–Sat 11am–6pm, Sun 2.30pm–6pm. Admission £1.10 adults, £0.55 children.

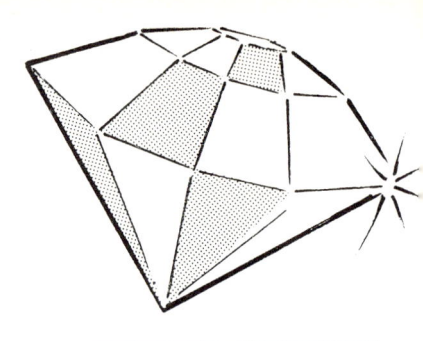

Diamond Centre

Did you know that a cut diamond always has 58 sides – no matter how big or how small? Well, the smallest diamond at the London Diamond Centre weighs only .008 carats and is tinier than a pinhead, yet it still has 58 sides. No wonder it takes 21 years to become a fully-fledged diamond cutter.

If you want to find out how a rough chunk of diamond is turned into a glittering jewel (and only one in four diamonds are of suitable quality, the rest are used in industry to make drilling and grinding tools) the tour here takes you right through the sequence of mining, sorting, cutting and polishing diamonds; there is even a display room where you can admire the finished results.

London Diamond Centre, 10 Hanover Street, London W1. Tel: 01-629 5511. Open Mon–Fri 9.30am–5.30pm, Sat 9.30am–1.30pm. Admission £2.45.

Dog's Cemetery

If you like your pets dead you may be weird, but you're not alone. More than 200 former dog owners obviously feel the same, since they've buried their dead mutts in great style in this cemetery in Kensington Gardens. Worth a visit if you like grave humour.

Dog's Cemetery, Kensington Gardens, London W2. Open daily. Admission free.

Express Dairies

We all drink it and we know it starts with grass and cows, but how does it get from there to our breakfast table? If you're curious to see the way milk is processed and distributed in London there's no better place to visit than the South Morden Dairy. Every day some 325,000 litres of milk flow through here as great bulk tankers bring it in straight from the 320 farms in southern England that supply the dairy. Next it is checked and pumped into huge silos, then pasteurized and sorted by variety (skimmed, homogenised, etc) into different bottles and cartons. You can stand on the balcony and watch as hundreds of bottles of milk a minute are filled, capped and crated automatically.

Express Dairies Milk Bottling Plant, 181 London Road, South Morden, Surrey. Tel: 01-648 4544. Tours start Mon–Fri 10am. Admission free (min. age 11 years).

Football Clubs

What football club has an underground station named after it, has never been out of the First Division in its history, and in the dim and distant past would fire a cannon before each game? If you're up on your football trivia you'll know it's Arsenal. If not, then a visit to the club will fill this empty crater in your knowledge.

The tour at Arsenal takes you round the stadium, the training centre, the pitch, and the Rooms (Dressing, Press and Board). You also get a short history of the club and a visit to the shop to buy football souvenirs.

TOURS & VISITS

A similar kind of tour can be found at Wembley Stadium, which any number of fans consider to be the most famous football venue in the galaxy.

Arsenal Football Stadium, Avenell Road, Highbury, London N5. Tel: 01-226 0304. Open Mon–Fri with tours at 10.30am (by appointment only). Admission free. Wembley Stadium, Wembley, Middlesex. Tel: 01-903 4864. Open daily except Thursday, tours every hour on the hour. Admission £2.50 adults, £1.50 children.

Ford Motor Company

The Ford factory at Dagenham is the biggest car plant in Europe; the entire site sprawls over 4.4 square kilometres and is the workplace for 18,500 people.

While it takes about 22.5 hours to build a car from start to finish, the tour itself is mercifully shorter. You won't be able to see a lot of the car-building process, although by the end of the tour you will have walked almost 5 kilometres in tiring conditions. Along the way you'll visit the Engine Plant, where 14 different kinds of engines are built, and the Press Shop, where the body shells of cars are made (here, much of the work is now done by robots). Farther along the assembly lines the cars are painted and their wheels, motor, seats, lights and other bits are fitted into place. Around 1000 cars a day roll off the end of the lines.

Ford Motor Company, Factory Tours, Dagenham Plant, Dagenham, Essex. Tel: 01-592 3000. Tours Mon–Fri, 9.45am & 1.30pm. Admission free (min. age 15).

Glasshouse

The Glasshouse is a shop and mini glass factory in Covent Garden. You can stand at the front and watch while craftsmen use the furnaces at the back to melt and blow beautifully coloured glass before working it into all sorts of wonderful shapes. Some of the pieces are on display and sale at the front of the shop, although racks more are stored in the basement.

The Glasshouse, 65 Long Acre, London WC2. Tel: 01-836 9785. Open Mon–Fri 10am–5pm, Sat 11am–4.30pm. Admission free.

Guinness World of Records

One of the most popular tourist venues in London is the World of Records where dozens of amazing facts from the Guinness Book of Records are on view. You'll find life-size models of the tallest and heaviest men, a model of the poor fellow who was hit seven times by lightning, and strange displays of the biggest, deepest, fastest and highest events, places, animals and people in the world. Amazing, and an education too.

Guinness World of Records, The Trocadero, Piccadilly Circus, London W1. Tel: 01-439 7331. Open 10am–10pm daily. Admission £2.80 adults, £1.80 children.

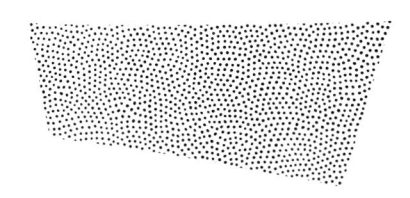

IBA Broadcasting Gallery

As you've probably suspected there's more to television than the on-off switch, but where do you go to find out about it?

Ever since 1968, the IBA has had a museum of radio and television broadcasting in Britain, with exhibits right from the earliest days. You'll find a mock-up of the Alexandra Palace studio, where the first regular TV broadcasts were made in November 1936. The camera used then was so heavy that it had to be bolted to the floor in case it toppled over; at the time there were only 400 television sets in the country to receive the broadcasts!

Here, too, is a display showing a TV newsroom at work as it covers a big story and races to get it on the air by news time, and there's also an exhibit of the way a studio drama is planned and put together.

A tour lasts about as long as two half-hour sitcoms.

IBA Broadcasting Gallery, 70 Brompton Road, London SW3. Tel: 01-584 7011. Open Mon–Fri, tours at 10am, 11am, 2pm, 3pm, booking essential. Admission free (min. age 16).

TOURS & VISITS

Lloyd's of London

For an institution that began life in a noisy coffee house Lloyd's has certainly come a long way. Today it is housed in a space-age building in the City, from where a large chunk of the world's insurance business is carried out.

Despite the hi-tech, you'll still be greeted by a 'waiter' when you go on a tour – the title dates from when Lloyd's was a coffee house in the 17th century, and the place to go to for maritime news and insurance deals.

As you ride up the glass lifts you'll have a great view of the surrounding City, while from the visitor's balcony you'll be able to peer down to the main Underwriting Room four floors below. Here, in the centre, is the famous Lutine Bell which is still rung when important news announcements are made – once for bad news and twice for good.

Lloyd's of London, Lime Street, London EC3. Tel: 01-623 7100. Open Mon–Fri 10am–4pm. Admission free (min. age 14), but phone first to book.

London Dungeon

Never be taken in by the politeness and nice manners of the English. All that Viking, Saxon and Celtic barbarian blood in them is never far beneath the skin, and if you need proof a visit to the London Dungeon should convince you. The dark vaults here contain a gruesome exhibition of life-size scenes of people being maimed, murdered, tortured, mutilated, executed and dealt with in innumerable grisly ways, all true and based on actual quaint British traditions of the Middle Ages.

If you'd like a revolting experience that'll put some colour in your nightmares, this is a great place to spend an afternoon. But don't go if you're squeamish (young kids and weak-kneed parents are advised not to be taken).

London Dungeon, 28–34 Tooley Street, London SE1. Tel: 01-403 0606. Open daily 10am–4.30pm. Admission £3.50 adults, £2.00 children.

TOURS & VISITS

Lord's Cricket Ground

If you think that cricket has something to do with small, noisy insects then you should give this place a miss. But if the sound of red leather on sprung willow makes your heart skip a beat then you're in for a real treat.

The tour that takes you around Lord's – the most famous cricket ground in the world – starts at Grace Gate, named after the legendary W. G. Grace, the 19th-century player who, single handed, made or broke more cricketing records than any player before or since. A short film outlines the history of cricket from its origins in a 13th-century game called trap ball, and includes the story of Thomas Lord, the wealthy Yorkshire wine merchant who formed the

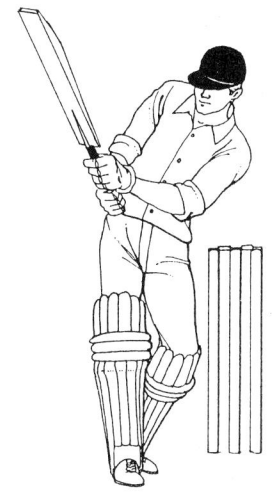

London Planetarium

Most people who look up at the night sky can tell you more about the crick in their neck than about the objects they are peering at. A great place to visit if you want to discover more about the stars and planets is the Planetarium. The half-hour show here is in an auditorium where you lie back in your seat and watch as the night sky is projected onto the huge dome above you. You can see the planets and constellations move about and, in a sequence in which time is speeded up, watch the Sun move through an entire day in a minute.

Outside the auditorium is the Astronomers' Gallery with displays about world-famous astronomers.

London Planetarium, Marylebone Road, London NW1. Tel: 01-486 1121. Open daily 11am–4.30pm. Admission £2.10 adults, £1.30 children.

TOURS & VISITS

Marylebone Cricket Club and bought the present site in 1814.

The tour lasts two hours, (nothing in cricket happens quickly) and it takes you through the Long Room with its elegant portraits of famous cricketers, and through the Memorial Gallery where exhibits show how the game has changed over the years. Here too, you'll see the urn holding The Ashes, and their origins will be explained (nothing to do with W. G. Grace for once!).

Lord's Cricket Ground, St John's Wood Road, London NW8. Tel: 01-289 1611. Open Oct–March, Mon–Fri 10am–5pm. Admission £0.50 adults, £0.25 children.

Madame Tussauds

One of the most popular places to visit in London, to judge by the queues at least, is this wax museum next to the London Planetarium. Inside you'll find some 350 figures of pop stars, sports personalities, royalty, politicians, criminals, murderers and other characters famous and infamous. The figures are life-size, and dressed with great attention to detail, right down to the buttons on their clothes, their hair-styles and footwear.

As well as a Chamber of Horrors with scenes recreating Jack the Ripper's grim murders, you'll also find a tableau of the Battle of Trafalgar, complete with smoke, noise, cannon fire and wounded sailors lying around the deck.

A great place to spend a wet afternoon, though the price of admission means you'll have to spend the whole afternoon here to make it good value.

Madame Tussauds, Marylebone Road, London NW1. Tel: 01-935 6861. Open daily 10am–5.30pm. Admission £3.70 adults, £2.10 children.

National Newspapers

Several of Britain's leading newspapers put on guided tours in the evenings just as the papers start going to press. The tours last 2–3 hours and take you everywhere, from the newsrooms to the presses.

The Daily Telegraph
Daily Mirror
Daily Mail
THE INDEPENDENT

Along the way you'll see every stage of the process of putting a national newspaper to bed. However, waiting lists for these tours are long, so apply in writing and expect a lengthy delay. Not something for the hurried tourist.

TOURS & VISITS

The Daily Mail, New Carmelite House, New Carmelite Street, London EC4. Tel: 01-353 6000 (ask for Production Manager). Admission free (min. age 14).

The Daily Express, 121 Fleet Street, London EC4. Tel: 01-353 8000 (ask for General Manager). Admission free.

National Theatre

Tours of the National Theatre last 1 hour 15 minutes and give you a chance to wander through the theatrical world hidden behind the scenes.

Visitors are taken through the three theatres of the complex – the Olivier, Lyttleton and Cottesloe. The largest, the Olivier, can hold an audience of almost 1200 people and the smallest, the Cottesloe, just 400. You may see a rehearsal taking place as you walk through, or a production being readied as sound and light checks are made and scenery is shifted about. You'll also have a chance to visit the prop stores, costume room and workshops.

As well as seeing the layout backstage you'll find out about such traditional theatrical rituals as sending first night good wishes cards and telling people to 'break a leg' for good luck. The National has its own ritual too that was started by Sir Ralph Richardson. On opening night, as the first lines of a new production are being spoken, a rocket (known as Ralph's Rocket) is fired from the roof.

National Theatre, South Bank, London SE1. Tel: 01-633 0880. Open Mon–Sat, tours 10.15am, 12.30pm, 12.45pm, 5.30pm, 6pm (phone to book). Admission £2.00 per person, £1.50 students.

Post Office

While a visit to the local Post Office on giro day is an ordeal you might prefer never to repeat, a trip to a main sorting office is an experience not to be missed.

There are two huge offices in London that handle much of the inland and overseas mail that gets sorted daily. The one at Mount Pleasant handles about three million letters a day, and is the biggest in Britain.

In the primary sorting area letters are bundled into batches, and those that are correctly addressed with a post code are sent along to the Code Sort section. Here the postcode is punched into a keyboard (there are 1.5 million codes in the country – one for every 37 people!) and a set of blue dots appears on the envelope. The envelopes are then read automatically and sorted by machine at a rate of 16,000 letters an hour. Badly addressed letters, known as blind letters, go to the Blind Duty Officer whose task it is to decipher the destination. Did you know that a letter to Newport (without the county) causes one of the biggest headaches of all, since there are 14 different Newports in the UK?

In the basement of the building you can see the automatic railway which carries 35,000 sacks of mail daily between seven different sorting offices and mainline stations from Paddington to Whitechapel.

Tours last about two hours. You can also visit the National Postal Museum where there are proof sheets of every British stamp since Penny Blacks were first issued back in 1840. The Museum has one of the biggest stamp collections in the world.

Mount Pleasant Sorting Office, Farringdon Road, London EC1. Tel: 01-239 2188. Tours Mon–Thurs, 10.30am, 2.30pm, 7pm (booking essential – minimum two week's notice). Admission free.

King Edward Building, 9 King Edward Street, London EC1. Tel: 01-239 5024. Tours Mon–Thurs, 10.30am, & 2.30pm (must book at least 10 days in advance). Admission free.

National Postal Museum, 8 King Edward Street, London EC1. Tel: 01-432 3851. Open Mon–Fri, 10am–4.30pm. Admission free.

Royal Opera House

The Opera House tour begins in the elegant foyer of this building and moves off into the huge auditorium where rows of red seats and thick plush carpets greet you. As you look up you'll be amazed by the ornate gilded ceiling high above and the rows of boxes. Generally speaking, boxes are expensive, but are great for holding snug private parties.

As the tour continues you climb up back stairs to look at the small private rooms where guests can be entertained in between acts of an opera or ballet, and go into the Royal Box where, among other things, you'll discover that the view isn't so great but that the box has its own side room where royalty retire to eat food served by their own staff.

Backstage you'll cross high catwalks and tour the cramped quarters of the workshops, wardrobes, dressing rooms and rehearsal rooms.

Royal Opera House, Bow Street, Covent Garden, London WC2. Tel: 01-240 1200. Tours Mon–Fri, 2.30pm only (must book). Admission £2.50, min. group is 16 people.

St Paul's Cathedral

One of the best views in the whole of London can be had from the Golden Gallery high on top of the dome of St Paul's; it's 111 hair-raising metres up and well worth the panting and red face needed to climb all the steps.

Failing that, there's a far less arduous climb to the Whispering Gallery on the inside of the dome, and from there you can easily step outside to the Stone Gallery at the base of the dome.

In the bowels of the church is the Crypt, which is open to visitors too.

A tour of the Cathedral takes two hours and barely seems to skim the surface of all the history and architectural splendour to be found here. As well as visiting the main building you'll also get a chance to see some of the small chapels and rooms that are not usually open to the public.

St Paul's Cathedral, Ludgate Hill, London EC4. Tel: 01-248 2705. Galleries open Mon–Sat, 10am–4.15pm (an hour less in winter). Admission £0.80 adults, £0.40 children.

TV Show Visits

If you'd like to join the crowd on a TV programme that has a live audience, all you need do is write in – well in advance – to the following addresses, letting them know which shows you'd like to see. Don't forget to enclose a stamped, self-addressed envelope in which the tickets can be sent to you. The tickets, you'll be glad to hear, are free.

For BBC programmes write to: Ticket Unit, BBC Broadcasting House, London W1.

For London Weekend shows write to: Ticket Office, LWT, Television Centre, South Bank, London SE1.

For Thames programmes write to: Ticket Office, Thames Television, 149 Tottenham Court Road, London W1.

TOURS & VISITS

Twickenham Football Ground

Twickenham is to rugby football what Hollywood is to movies – home. Fans come here as if on pilgrimage, but even if your notion of rugby players is of a load of beer-swilling maniacs rolling in the mud, a tour of the grounds is well worth the trip.

Rugby is another one of those Great British Inventions that was taught to the world and is now often played far better elsewhere than here – though the best museum is still in this country. The tour at Twickenham starts with a short film of an important international match and then continues with a visit to the museum itself. Here the history of the modern game, from the school where it was invented (Rugby) until the present is traced. Afterwards you go around the grounds and the stands, visit the players' dressing rooms and inspect the Committee Lounge where you can pretend to be a rugby bigwig as you take in all the portraits, trophies and club crests hanging here.

Rugby Football Union, Twickenham, TW1 1DZ. Tel: 01-892 8161. Tours Mon–Fri, 10.30am & 2.15pm (booking essential). Admission £1.00 adults, £0.50 children.

Westminster Abbey

Ever since William the Conqueror was crowned here on Christmas Day in 1066, the Abbey has been the setting for the coronation of English kings and queens. It has also been the burial place for many of them, and also what seems like half the entire royal family – brothers, sisters and cousins too. Some 5000 people have been laid to rest here and the resulting shortage of space has

TOURS & VISITS

even led to such bizarre solutions as burying one poet (Ben Jonson) standing up.

Tombs and monuments fill every inch of the Abbey. In Poet's Corner are the remains of Chaucer and memorials to Milton, Shakespeare, Keats, Wordsworth, Eliot and others. In Statesman's Aisle there are statues of various ex-prime ministers, while Henry VIII's chapel is completely festooned with the banners and crests of the Knights of the Order of the Bath, making this the most colourful corner of the Abbey.

If you go on a tour you'll get a chance to see the Royal Chapels and Abbey Treasure, not to mention Nelson's Hat, the oldest stuffed parrot in England (which once belonged to the Duchess of Richmond), the Coronation Chair (complete with graffitti carved by the boys of Westminster School) and replicas of the Crown Jewels. It needs several visits to begin to take it all in, but remember, the Abbey gets very crowded in tourist season.

Westminster Abbey, Parliament Square, London SW1. Tel: 01-222 7110. Open Mon–Fri 9am–4.30pm, Sat 9am–2pm and 4pm–5pm. Admission free to the nave, but visits to Royal Chapels, Tombs & Treasures cost £1.60 adults, £0.40 children. Guided tours, six daily in summer, four daily in winter, £3.50 per person.

Whitbread Stables

The shire horses stabled here are real working horses. They earn their keep hauling wagonloads of beer around the streets of London as they make deliveries to pubs. The shires are so spectacular to watch, and the drays they pull so brightly painted, that they make a terrific walking advertisement for their employers' beer.

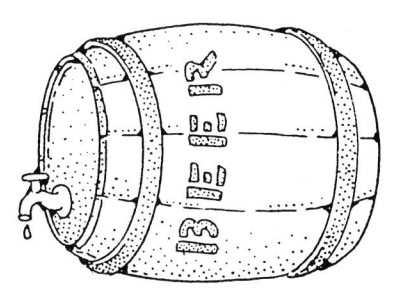

When you visit the stables you'll be going into a real sawdust strewn workplace (so dress accordingly) where you can see these gentle giants being fed and cleaned and, with luck, watch an old-fashioned blacksmith make shoes for them at his forge.

Whitbread Brewery Stables, Garrett Street, London EC1. Tel: 01-606 4455 ext 2534. Visits Mon–Fri, 11am–12.30pm, 1.30pm–3pm. Admission free for under 16s, otherwise £0.50 per person.

Galleries & Museums

If you devoted a lifetime to exploring London's galleries and museums, you'd probably have to be re-incarnated to finish the job. For visitors choice is never the problem – only time. Here are a few, to get you started.

Bethnal Green Museum of Childhood

'Not quite as good as a toy shop – but almost' would be a good description of this museum. You can't buy anything, but you certainly can look at one of the best collections of Dinky toys, metal and plastic toys, games, dolls, doll's houses, costumes and other wonderful things. There's even a museum shop where you can pick up replicas of old-fashioned games and toys.

Bethnal Green Museum of Childhood, Cambridge Heath Road, London E2. Tel: 01-980 2415. Open Mon–Sat, 10am–6pm, Sun 2.30pm–6pm, closed Fri. Admission free.

British Motor Museum

The British Motor Museum has the biggest collection of British cars anywhere, with some 100 models tracing the history of car building in this country from an 1895 Wolseley up to the present. There are also record-breaking cars on display, and prototypes that never made it into production.

On weekends during the summer there are free rides in some of the old cars.

British Motor Industry Heritage Trust, Syon Park, Brentford, Middlesex TW8. Tel: 01-560 1378. Open daily 10am–5.30pm (4pm in winter). Admission £1.60 adults, £0.90 children.

GALLERIES & MUSEUMS

British Museum

One of the great museums of the world, the BM is so big, and its collections cover such a vast range of material that it's really useful to pick up a copy of the children's guide called *Inside the British Museum* (£1.20) to help you get started.

As you walk around you'll find room after room of relics from ancient Egypt, Greece and Rome as well as smaller collections from China and India, while the British section covers man-made objects from prehistoric times to the late Middle Ages. A very popular place to start a visit is with the collection of Egyptian mummies and papyrus drawings.

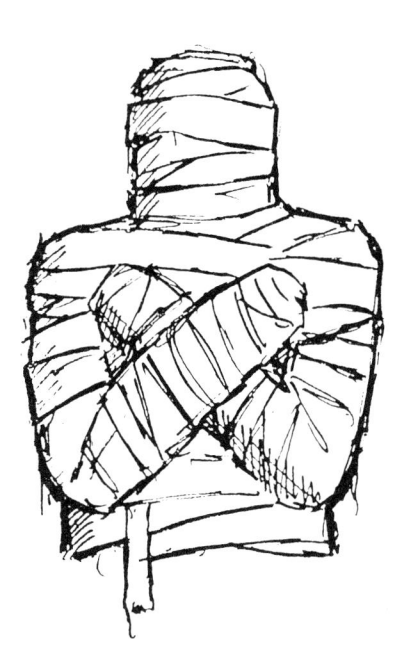

In the library over 176 kilometres of shelves and 10 million books are stored, but these are not available to the general public unless you have a special reader's pass to get in.

On school holidays there are special talks and activities for children aged 8 to 13. Phone for details.

British Museum, Great Russell Street, London WC1. Tel: 01-636 1555. Open Mon–Sat 10am–5pm, Sun 2.30pm–6pm. Admission free.

Cabinet War Rooms

This underground bunker was built to let Churchill, his war cabinet and the chiefs of the armed forces survive and work through air raids during the war. The 19 rooms were in constant use from 1939 to 1945, with over 100 cabinet meetings held down here during this time. The equipment, machines, maps and furniture are all preserved just as they were left when World War II came to an end.

Cabinet War Rooms, Clive Steps, King Charles Street, London SW1. Tel: 01-930 6961. Open daily, 10am–5.15pm. Admission £2.50 adults, £1.15 children.

GALLERIES & MUSEUMS

Commonwealth Institute

This odd-looking building always has displays and exhibitions from all of the countries that make up the Commonwealth, and which represent almost a quarter of the population of the world under one roof! Here you can see, among other things, a transparent milk-producing cow from New Zealand, a tropical climate simulator from Malaysia and a Wild West saddle and a skidoo (open snowmobile) from Canada.

On weekends and school holidays there are special events for kids; films, plays, story-telling, mime, masks, puppets, music, costumes and much more.

Commonwealth Institute, Kensington High Street, London W8. Tel: 01-603 4535. Open Mon–Sat 10am–5.30pm, Sun 2pm–5pm. Admission free.

Geffrye Museum

In this small museum are a series of rooms that have been decorated in period styles from the 1600s to 1939, and which show how homes looked in the past. Each one of the nine rooms is typical of the way we once lived. They start at a time when hardly anyone owned much furniture (back in the days when a single chair made do for a whole household) to a world in which objects seem to clutter every corner of our living rooms.

Every Saturday, and on school holidays, the museum holds activity workshops for kids, based around themes such as clothing, hair styles, make-up, dirt, running water and other items from daily life.

Geffrye Museum, Kingsland Road, London E2. Tel: 01-739 8368. Open Tues–Sat 10am–5pm, Sun 2–5pm. Admission free.

Geological Museum

A huge museum in which you'll find a massive collection of rocks, gems and fossils that you can explore for hours. One really spectacular gem is the

GALLERIES & MUSEUMS

Crystal of Tourmaline which comes from California. There's also a chunk of Moon rock that was brought back by astronauts on the Apollo 16 mission.

But the most impressive displays by half are of a mini-volcano and an earthquake generator. This is actually a moving platform that you can stand on to experience being in a real tremor (not unlike riding in a badly maintained lift). There are film shows too, and special activities that run during school holidays

Geological Museum, Exhibition Road, London SW7. Tel: 01-589 3444. Open Mon–Sat 10am–6pm, Sun 2.30–6pm. Admission free.

Horniman Museum

The Horniman comes as close as anything to the ideal of a small but perfectly formed museum. Tucked away in Forest Hill, south London, it is crammed with fascinating artefacts (a polite word for antique arts and crafts from the third world) from Asia, the Pacific, South America and Africa, not to mention musical instruments and a huge range of natural history – both alive and stuffed.

The collections here grew out of Frederick J Horniman's over-developed hoarding instincts. He was a tea magnate who travelled the world filling his pockets, and then crates, with countless souvenirs until he finally had enough to fill a museum. His private collection is what you see when you visit here (the museum was founded in the 1890s).

Along with Egyptian mummies and masks from the Pacific you'll find a stuffed walrus and ostrich, a vivarium with snakes and lizards, a working beehive under glass, tropical fish and much more. Free lectures and courses are also held, as are concerts and children's activities on weekends and holidays.

Horniman Museum, 100 London Road, Forest Hill, London SE23. Tel: 01-699 2339. Open Mon–Sat 10.30am–6pm, Sun 2pm–6pm. Admission free.

GALLERIES & MUSEUMS

Imperial War Museum

This place should be known as 'a heavy metal museum' because that, at heart, is what warfare in the 20th century is all about – heavy machines flinging lumps of metal about. You'll really get the feel for this as you walk up to the entrance past two huge fifteen-inch naval guns weighing 100 tonnes each.

Inside the museum are displays of planes, tanks, artillery, armoured vehicles, uniforms, medals, posters, propaganda, documents, photos, and paintings by official war artists that tell the story of war from 1914 to today. There is a display showing how the *Dambusters* raid was carried out, not to mention the London bus known as *Old Bill* which was used to carry troops to the front line in World War I. There is even a collection of miniature models of fighting ships and planes.

On weekends and school holidays there are free showings of documentary films.

Imperial War Museum, Lambeth Road, London SE1. Tel: 01-735 8922. Open Mon–Sat 10am–5.30pm, Sun 2pm–5.30pm. Admission free.

Kew Bridge Engines Trust

One of the things that really sets old-fashioned engines apart from modern ones is size. In the past lots of power meant lots of bulk, and nothing proves this more than the two huge beam engines of the Kew Bridge steam museum. The older was built in 1820 and between them they are the largest steam engines in the world.

They were used for years to pump water from the Thames into London's reservoir system. Nowadays, restored to working order in a vast Victorian pumping station, the beam engines are steamed up each weekend for the benefit of the public.

Kew Bridge Steam Museum, Green Dragon Lane, Brentford, Middlesex. Tel: 01-568 4757. Open Sat & Sun 11am–5pm. Admission £1.60 adults, £0.80 children.

GALLERIES & MUSEUMS

London Fire Brigade Museum

Not many people know this but one of the ways of fighting fires in the past was with fire grenades. They usually halted the conflagration, but made a terrific mess of the premises.

If you'd like to see these and other items of fire-fighting gear from the 17th century to the present, take a trip over the Southwark Bridge to the Fire Brigade Museum. Here you'll see the leather buckets that firemen in the past carried with them, as well as uniforms, medals and insurance company fire marks. In the War Room at the top of the museum are two unexploded bombs from World War II – now safely defused.

London Fire Brigade Museum, 94a Southwark Bridge Road, London SE1. Tel: 01-587 4273. Open Mon–Fri 10am–4pm (must book). Admission free.

London Toy & Model Museum

If grown-up toys – like cars and planes and boats – all have museums built for them, why shouldn't children's toys get the same treatment? Well, at last they have, at the Toy and Model Museum. This building is crammed with tiny wonders – old tin toys (originally all priced at one penny), models, fire engines, dolls, stuffed animals – just about everything you've ever wanted to get your hands on but didn't have enough birthdays or Christmases to collect.

Down in the garden of the museum is a miniature steam railway that you can ride and a boating pool and flight simulator. In the lower gallery there's a diorama called the 'City at Night' which lights up very convincingly (but for which there is an extra charge), while some of the other exhibits are working models that you can actually get your hands on and play with – which is the whole point of toys really.

The London Toy & Model Museum, 21/23 Craven Hill, London W2. Tel: 01-262 7905. Open Tues–Sat 10am–5.30pm, Sun 11am–5pm. Admission £1.50 adults, £0.50 children.

111

GALLERIES & MUSEUMS

London Transport Museum

Here's a chance to play in the traffic without breaking any rules or giving the rest of the world a heart-attack – for in this case the traffic is standing still in a museum. Here you can sit in the driver's seat of a London double-decker, jump on and off a tram and examine horse-drawn buses that were used over a century ago. There are also displays that show how the transport system of London manages to move millions of people a day in and out of town (mostly without too much chaos).

London Transport Museum, The Piazza, Covent Garden, London WC2. Tel: 01-379 6344. Open daily 10am–6pm. Admission £2.00 adults, £1.00 children.

Museum of Garden History

The English, it is said, are passionate about their pets and their gardens, but fairly off-hand about each other. The upshot is that English gardens are glorious places to visit but don't expect anybody to talk to you while you're there. Here in the grounds of the former church of St Mary-at-Lambeth, The Tradescant Trust has created a beautiful garden-museum filled with rare and interesting plants.

The Museum is just across the river from the Houses of Parliament, right next to the gates of Lambeth Palace. Inside you'll find an exhibition which describes the history of gardening and gardeners since the 17th century, when new and unusual flowers, shrubs and trees from all over the world first began to be brought into England in large numbers by travelling collectors – two of the best known being the

THYME   PARSLEY   BASIL

GALLERIES & MUSEUMS

Tradescants father and son (after whom the trust is named).

Unless you're really up on garden plants the best way to see this museum and garden is with one of the museum's guides. Write or phone well in advance.

Museum of Garden History, St Mary-at-Lambeth, Lambeth Road, London SE1. Tel: 01-261 1891. Open Mar to mid-Dec, Mon–Fri 11am–3pm, Sun 10.30am–5pm. Admission free.

Museum of London

London is almost 2000 years old – and on bad days looks it! – though in fact very little of what you see now dates back more than 200 or 300 years.

But the Museum of London does a terrific job of describing the city's history, right from the time it was a boggy little Roman fort on the north side of the Thames. You'll be able to inspect the actual foundations of the Roman and Medieval wall that ringed the city, see the devastation of the Great Fire, look at models of Victorian shops and trace the spread of the suburbs as they engulfed hundreds of villages during the 19th and 20th century.

Museum of London, London Wall, London EC2. Tel: 01-600 3699. Open Tues–Sat 10am–6pm, Sun 2pm–6pm. Admission free.

Museum of Mankind

Here you'll find exhibitions showing the life-styles of non-Western societies. You'll be able to inspect costumes, homes, crafts, art and even sample the sounds and smells of these people's lives. Heady stuff!

Museum of Mankind, 6 Burlington Gardens, London W1. Tel: 01-437 2224. Open Mon–Sat 10am–5pm, Sun 2.30pm–6pm. Admission free.

National Army Museum

A permanent British army was first established in 1485; prior to that wars were fought by makeshift groups of soldiers who would disband after each campaign.

The fascinating story of the regular army can be found here along with displays of uniforms, arms, armour and regimental colours (not to mention the skeleton of Napoleon's horse 'Marengo').

National Army Museum, Royal Hospital Road, London SW3. Tel: 01-730 0717. Open Mon–Sat 10am–5.30pm, Sun 2pm–5.30pm. Admission free.

GALLERIES & MUSEUMS

National Maritime Museum

This is the place to find out about England's sea-faring tradition, from prehistoric days when people bobbed about on logs to a navy of sail-driven men-of-war and today's modern missile-carrying ships.

There are hundreds of model ships to admire, and life-size ones too, and a fabulous collection of charts, maps, telescopes and sextants used by sailors to work out their position at sea. All sorts of naval paraphernalia including uniforms and weapons, as well as paintings of derring-do on the high seas complete the exhibition here.

Next door is the Old Royal Observatory where you can straddle the brass line marking longitude zero and also examine a collection of telescopes and chronometers.

National Maritime Museum, Romney Road, Greenwich, London SE10. Tel: 01-858 4422. Open Mon–Sat 10am–6pm, Sun 2pm–6.30pm (an hour less late in winter). Admission £1.50 adults, £0.75 children.

Natural History Museum

The animals you'll see here are all as dead as a dodo – you'll even be able to find out just how dead that is by visiting the bird gallery – they've got a dodo there that isn't just deceased – it's extinct.

You'll have a chance to compare both ends of the animal kingdom spectrum with a model of the biggest mammal of all, the blue whale (that's next to impossible to miss) and, hidden somewhere, a pygmy white-toothed shrew (you'll probably have to ask someone to point it out). But the main attractions here are the dinosaur skeletons and life-size models. Did you know, for instance, that at 14 metres the tail of the *Diplodocus* is as long as three medium-sized cars?

On the other hand, it should make your skin crawl to learn that there are over a million different types of (dead) insects kept in this museum.

During the summer and spring holidays you can visit the Family Centre where you can touch a python's skin (with no python in it), examine a butterfly's wings under a microscope, make a cast of a dinosaur's footprint and try all sorts of experiments as you explore the subject of natural history.

Natural History Museum, Cromwell Road, London SW7. Tel: 01-589 6323. Open Mon–Sat 10am–6pm, Sun 2.30pm–6pm. Admission free.

Old Operating Theatre

In one corner of Guy's Hospital, just south of the Thames, is a restored 19th-century operating theatre. It's the only one of its kind to survive from the days when antiseptics were unknown – so if you were a patient here forget sterile.

The theatre was built in 1821 and used for 40 years before being bricked up and forgotten until 1956. It was opened again to the public 100 years after it was last used for surgery.

Nearby is a herb garret where medicinal herbs were dried and stored. There is also an exhibition here which tells you about pharmacy, nursing and surgery in the 19th century.

Old St Thomas' Operating Theatre & Herb Garret, Guy's Hospital, St Thomas Street, London SE1. Tel: 01-407 7600 ext 2739. Open Mon, Wed, Fri 12.30pm–4pm. Admission £0.70 adults, £0.35 children.

Pollock's Toy Museum

Although the oldest toy in here is 4000 years old, and there's an 82-year-old teddy bear too, this tiny museum has only been around since 1956. It spreads over two buildings crammed to bursting with dolls, doll's houses, teddies, tin toys, games, comics, jigsaws (invented in the 1700s), puppets and modern space toys too. But some of the most famous games here are the toy theatres that were immensely popular in the 1800s; children used them to stage performances with cardboard characters and real scripts.

Pollock's Toy Museum, 1 Scala Street, London W1. Tel: 01-636 3452. Open Mon–Sat 10am–5pm. Admission £0.60 adults, £0.30 children.

GALLERIES & MUSEUMS

Royal Air Force Museum

This museum, and the Battle of Britain and Bomber Command Museums next door, is on the site of an old airfield, and all the exhibits are in former hangars. If you have a thing about planes you'll be in heaven here, where you can view everything from tiny pre-World War I monoplanes to supersonic Tornados, front line attack craft in service today. But the most spectacular and romantic planes of all (to our way of thinking) are the beautiful flying boats.

Royal Air Force Museum, Grahame Park Way, Hendon, London NW9. Tel: 01-205 2266. Open Mon–Sat, 10am–6pm, Sun 2pm–6pm. Admission is free, but there's a charge for the Battle of Britain Museum.

Science Museum

As a description 'jam-packed' doesn't do justice to this place where, spread over five floors, you'll find just about every invention you've ever heard of – and a lot you probably haven't. On display is everything from atom-smashers to zip-fasteners including a mock-up of the lunar module of Apollo 11. Elsewhere the story of the ballpoint pen vies with the history of steam locomotives. You can examine an amateur radio station that actually works, try out the 'hands-on' experiments of the Launch Pad exhibition or discover how much plastic goes into a modern car. Even if you had a week to explore the place you'd still have a lot to come back for.

On Saturday afternoons and school holidays there are free demonstrations, lectures and films. A mega-treat!

Science Museum, Exhibition Road, London SW7. Tel: 01-589 3456. Open Mon–Sat 10am–6pm, Sun 2.30pm–6pm. Admission free (but as the donation machine tells you, 10p helps run the museum for 1.1 seconds).

Tate Gallery

This beautiful building overlooking the Thames has the best collection of 19th and 20th century pictures in Britain, one that anyone in their right mind would give anything to have hanging on their walls.

Obviously you can't, but you can always buy cards and posters in the museum shop of paintings by the likes of Hogarth, Blake, Constable and the Pre-Raphaelites and pin them up instead. Off to one side is the newly-opened Clore Gallery that houses the Turner collection and which, for some reason, always seems to be full

GALLERIES & MUSEUMS

of French tourists.

On school holidays there are tours and quizzes to introduce kids to the collection.

Tate Gallery, Millbank, London SW1. Tel: 01-821 1313. Open Mon–Sat 10am–6pm, Sun 2pm–6pm. Admission free (but special exhibitions have charges).

Telecom Technology Showcase

If you are under the impression that the phone system is just public boxes and a new Mickey Mouse-style model in the hall then you're in for a shock. There's a lot more to telecommunications than meets the eye, as you'll discover here, and most of it is hidden under the streets in cables, up in the sky in satellites, and in computers and phone exchanges around the country. The phone system is very, very BIG – in this country alone there are 23 million customers.

There's a history of the phone system too, from the days when operators put every call through by hand (and when the first phone system – in 1879 – had only ten subscribers) to the latest gadgets with video screens, computer memory and the rest. You can also handle some of the exhibits, and even send a local telex.

Telecom Technology Showcase, 135 Queen Victoria Street, London EC4. Tel: 01-248 7444. Open Mon–Fri 10am–5pm. Admission free.

Theatre Museum

This shiny new museum, the first of its kind in the UK, opened most fittingly on 23 April 1987 – Shakespeare's birthday! It is home to a wonderful exhibition of the performing arts, starting with costumes and objects from the first public theatres in the 16th century, and including material from the circus and the opera, not to mention mime, Punch & Judy, panto, music hall, ballet, dance and pop music costume and makeup.

Theatre Museum, Russell Street, London WC2E 7PA. Tel: 01-836 4648. Open Tues–Sat 11am–8pm, Sun 11am–7pm. Admission £2.25 adults, £1.25 children, under fives free.

Shops & Markets

Napoleon once called the English 'a nation of shopkeepers'. He meant it as an insult but we seem to have taken it as a compliment. Certainly nobody running a shop or stall in London today would argue with him. As well as shops that sell everything under the sun, London has a long tradition of street markets where traders stock everything from antiques to zips. There are huge wholesale markets too where the public can't buy, although it can come to watch the professionals at work.

Balloons

Any type of balloons – rubber, metallic, and even specially printed ones with your own message or design can be bought here. They'll even blow them up for you on the spot.

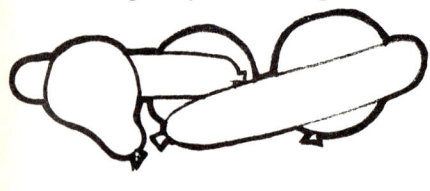

Balloons, Bouquets, Candygrams, 82 Shaftesbury Avenue, London W1. Tel: 01-434 3039. Open Mon–Sat 10am–7pm.

Beatties

For anything to do with model trains and railways make tracks to this emporium. Beatties also stocks a great range of model kits of cars, planes, ships.

Beatties, 202 High Holborn, London WC1. Tel: 01-405 6285. Open Mon–Sat 10am–6pm.

Billingsgate Fish Market

A huge, modern fish market that opened in 1982 when the old market moved from its ancient site in the City of

London. If your idea of fun is getting up at 5am to stand around watching busy traders handling cold wet fish, then this is just the plaice for you. It's a wholesale market, so you won't be able to buy.

Billingsgate Market, North Quay, West India Dock Road, Isle of Dogs, London E14. Open Tues–Sat 5am–10am.

Bookshops

London has enough bookshops to merit a guidebook devoted just to them. It's impossible to list every one, although among the shoal in Charing Cross Road there are several with good children's departments.

Three places with some of the best or biggest children's sections are:

Children's Book Centre (said to have the largest selection in the UK), 229 Kensington High Street, London W8. Open Mon–Sat 9.30am–6pm.

Foyle's (possibly the most chaotic selection to get lost in), 119 Charing Cross Road, London W2. Open 9.30am–6pm.

Dillon's Bookstore (could be the cosiest selection to hide in), 1 Malet Street, London WC1. Open Mon–Sat 9am–5.30pm.

Camden Lock Market

Sprawling around a set of locks on the Regent's Canal, this weekend market has made a name for itself with the imaginative native crafts (native to Britain that is) and ethnic goods (jewellery, leatherware, carvings, pottery, herbs and oils) it sells. The quality is very high, the prices mostly reasonable, and among the hundreds of stalls there are enough selling food to keep even the most committed nibblers happy. Over the canal and down Camden High Street 100 metres is Camden Town Flea Market – good for records, clothes and jewellery.

Camden Lock Market, Camden Lock, London NW1. Open Sat–Sun 9am–6pm.

Camping Gear

While you don't see many pitched tents in Hyde Park, or people back-packing with compasses through the City there are a number of good shops in the middle of town selling camping gear to Londoners who can't wait to get into the country to do battle with nature (and the weather). Whenever you need a map or a sleeping bag try one of the following.

Blacks, 53 Rathbone Place,

SHOPS & MARKETS

London W1 or 10 Holborn, London EC1. Open Mon–Sat 10am–5.30pm.

Pindisports, 14 Holborn, London EC1. Open 9.30am–6pm.

Camping & Outdoor Centre, 124 Newgate Street, London EC1. Open Mon–Fri 9am–5.30pm.

Carnaby Street

For over 20 'trendy' years this street has been synonymous with fashion. Originally the street was the home of showbiz tailors who made clothes to order for the mods of the early 60s. As the dedicated followers of fashion began to hang out here other shops soon opened too. Today the flavour of the place is best found in stores like *Cascades* with its kicking legs in the window, and jokes, souvenirs and clothing inside.

Carnaby Street, London W1. Open Mon–Sat, usual hours.

Columbia Road Market

A place for gardeners and plant bargain hunters. This East End market has trays and pots of flowers and plants – and other gardener's gear – placed in boxes all across the road, making this a great place to browse in the street. Best bargains are around lunchtime.

Columbia Road Market, Shoreditch, London E2. Open Sun 9am–1.30pm.

Comics

Everything from Action Comics to ZAP Comix, English, American and Euro – new and secondhand – can be found in these three well-stocked shops in the West End. They're a haven for comic fans from school age to retirement age, all of whom seem to be dedicated to a sport called 'marathon browsing' – and at a level almost worthy of its own Olympic event.

Comic Showcase, 76 Neal Street, London WC2. Open Mon–Sat 10am–6pm.

Forbidden Planet, 23 Denmark Street, London WC2. Open Mon–Sat 10am–6pm.

Gosh!, 39 Great Russell Street, London WC1. Open Mon–Sat 10am–6pm, Sun 1pm–6pm.

Computers

Lots of high-street chain shops now sell computers, although their selection of software is usually pretty limited. But the heart and soul of London's computer world is Tottenham Court Road, where dozens of shops vie with each other to sell computers, printers and other electronic gear. So long as you're looking for a computer that you can carry out of the door, you're sure to find it here. Start at the Oxford Street end and work your way up the road.

One shop of particular interest is *Pilot Software*, just off Tottenham Court Road, which stocks nothing but games and business software; the staff seem to know everything there is to know about the software they sell – which is fairly unusual.

Pilot Software, 32 Rathbone Place, London W1. Open Mon–Sat 9.30am–6pm.

Costumes

One of the best places to find amazing odds and ends of clothing is in a shop called *Laurence Corner*. What started out as a single army surplus store has now spread down the street and includes a costume shop, a hat shop and an utter junk shop. Most of the stuff is secondhand, but it's usually possible to find things still in good nick.

Laurence Corner, Hampstead Road, London N1.

Doll's House

A shop selling traditional doll's houses – and all their contents. You can buy a table and chair or a whole fully-furnished house either ready made or in kit form. The houses aren't exactly cheap, but it's always worth a visit if you want to look.

The Doll's House, 29 The Market, Covent Garden, London WC2. Tel: 01-379 7243. Open Mon–Sat 10am–8pm.

SHOPS & MARKETS

Games

If your idea of play is rolling dice, breaking the bank and getting lost in a dungeon then you'll want to go to places that specialize in board games. While most toy shops carry the standard board games we all know and love, the following stock everything under the sun.

Virgin Games Centre, 22 Oxford Street, London W1. Tel: 01-637 7911. Open Mon–Fri 10am–7pm, Sat 10am–6pm.

Hamley's Toy Shop (below).

Gifts

Anything bought in a shop or market could – in theory – be a gift, although a nicely-wrapped potato won't exactly win you any new friends. Given that the only honest definition of a gift is 'something wrapped up that I'd like to receive' here are a few West End places that stock the sorts of things we think most people like to be given.

Covent Garden General Store 111 Long Acre, London WC2. Tel: 01-240 0331. Open Mon–Sat 10am–midnight, Sun 11am–7pm.

Neal Street (the whole street seems to specialize in shops selling the kind of odds and ends that people like to get as presents), London WC2.

Paperchase, 213 Tottenham Court Road, London W1. Tel: 01-580 8496. Open Mon–Sat 9am–6pm.

Hamley's

The biggest toy shop in the universe is the way Hamley's likes to see itself, and if you go there on a Saturday in December the universe is who you'll meet here. There are five floors to get lost in, so come prepared to exhaust yourself.

Hamleys, 188–196 Regent Street, London W1. Tel: 01-734 3161. Open Mon–Thurs 9am–5.30pm, Fri–Sat 9am–8pm.

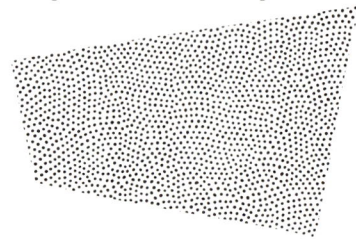

SHOPS & MARKETS

Hyper-Hyper

Across the street from Kensington Market is another indoor market devoted to fashion – clothes, make-up, hats, accessories – all of it new and original, and produced by young designers who are trying out new ideas. The range of styles is amazing.

Hyper-Hyper, 26–40 Kensington High Street, London W8. Open Mon–Sat 10am–6pm.

Jokes, Tricks & Magic

For some people the idea of a joke runs along the lines of sweets that turn your mouth bright blue, huge rubber teeth and whoopee cushions. If that sort of thing makes you split your sides there are a few shops in London that will happily cater to your tastes.

Davenport's, one of the best of them, also does a line in magic tricks and props if that's what you're interested in. They even have a stage with video cameras where you can practise and tape your act once you've joined their club.

Davenports Magic Shop, 7 Charing Cross Underground Concourse, London WC2. Tel: 01-836 0408. Open Mon–Fri 9.30am–5.30pm, Sat close at 4pm.

Alan Alan's Magic Spot, 88 Southampton Row, London WC1. Tel: 01-242 2235. Open Mon–Fri 10am–6pm, Sat 10am–2pm.

Kensington Market

This indoor market is a mecca for half the kids who ever visit London. It's packed with stalls selling new and secondhand clothes from Victorian uniforms to frocks from the 1930s and every youth style there's ever been since the 1950s. There are jewellers too, and stalls selling shoes and other odd bits and pieces.

Kensington Market, Kensington High Street, London W8. Open Mon–Sat 10am–6pm.

Kites

You can fly kites from rooftops or hilltops in London, but the best place to buy them is at a small specialist shop in Covent Garden that stocks every kind of kite imaginable. They range in price from small models at less than £5 to an enormous Flexifoil Hyper model that sells for £250. Along with kites you can find frisbees, boomerangs and mini hot-air balloons too.

The Kite Store, 69 Neal Street, London WC2 Tel: 01-836 1666. Open Mon–Fri 10.30am–6pm, Sat 10.30am–5pm.

Leadenhall Market

The nearest thing London has to a gourmet food fair is this covered market in the City. Underneath a magnificent iron and glass arcade the chefs for stockbrokers' dining rooms, as well as office workers from the area, come to shop. Alongside the poultry, flowers, cheese and vegetables is a selection of game and seafood just as impressive as that found in Harrods' Food Halls.

Leadenhall Market, Gracechurch Street, London EC3. Open Mon–Fri 11am–2pm.

Markets

Individual markets are listed alphabetically along with their opening times and details about what they are best known for. At retail markets the public can buy, but wholesale ones are for watching only – this is where professional traders and buyers do business.

Retail Markets: Camden Lock, Columbia Road, Kensington Market, Leadenhall, New Caledonian, Petticoat Lane, Portobello Road.

Wholesale Markets: Billingsgate, Borough, New Covent Garden, Smithfield, Spitalfields.

Model Shops

There's a big range of shops all across London selling models and model-kits for making planes, ships and trains; a few even specialize in one particular

SHOPS & MARKETS

range of models.

Aeronautical Models, 39 Parkway, London NW1 (Camden Town). Tel: 01-485 1818. Open Tues–Sat 9.15am–5.30pm.

Beatties (see separate listing).

Hamleys (see separate listing).

Model Railways Co., 14 York Way, London N1. (Specializes in rail and road transport models). Tel: 01-837 5551. Open Mon-Sat 9.30am–5.30pm.

Musical Instruments

If you ever want to form a band, or start playing an instrument professionally, chances are you'll end up browsing the shops along London's own 'Tin Pan Alley' – Denmark Street – where you can check out the keyboards and guitars, and get your first shock at music business prices. The whole area around here, especially along Charing Cross Road and Shaftesbury Avenue, is dotted with shops selling instruments and sheet music.

Allbang & Strummit, 22 Earlham Street, London WC2. Tel: 01-379 5142. Open Mon–Sat 10am–6pm.

Andy's Guitar Workshop, Rod Argent's Keyboards, Drumshop, Guitar Grapevine, Rhodes Music Company, Rhythm Box, Sho-Bud Steel Guitars; all found in Denmark Street, London WC2.

New Caledonian Market

Also known as Bermondsey Market this is the biggest regular antiques market in the south of England. Mainly it's a place where dealers come to buy and sell to each other, often snapping up the entire contents of a van at a time, paid for with wads of big notes. But there's all sorts of stuff for the general collector too; furniture, jewellery, watches, silverware, pottery, and all the other bits of bric-a-brac with which we clutter up our lives.

New Caledonian Market, Bermondsey Square, Tower Bridge Road, London SE1. Open Fridays 6am–11am.

SHOPS & MARKETS

New Covent Garden

Two busy wholesale markets where people in the fruit 'n' veg business and the flower trade buy their produce. Business in the former is fast and furious and you stand a fair-to-middling chance of being run down by porters with their over-loaded barrows. The flower market is friendlier (and less chilly). Both need to be visited very early in the morning – by 10am they're deserted.

New Covent Garden Fruit, Vegetable & Flower Market, Nine Elms Lane, London SW8. Open Mon–Fri 5am–10am.

Petticoat Lane

The most famous street market in England erupts over several streets on the fringes of London's East End every Sunday – not one of which is called Petticoat Lane (which is just a local nickname for Middlesex Street, deriving from a Yiddish word for the old clothes dealers who originally gathered here).

The market stall-holders seem to get as much fun out of being in the middle of all the noise and bustle as do local shoppers and tourists. You can buy just about everything here from bargain jewellery to used bathtubs.

Petticoat Lane, Aldgate, London E1. Open Sunday morning 9am–1.30pm.

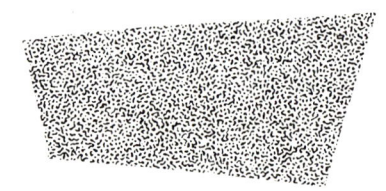

Portobello Road Market

Every Saturday the whole length of Portobello Road is transformed into a fabulous outdoor street market, with antiques stalls up at one end selling silverware, jewellery and clothing; food stalls in the middle and jumble and general bric-a-brac stalls under the flyover. The shops on both sides of the street and in side-streets are just as fascinating as the market itself.

Portobello Road, Notting Hill Gate, London W11. Open Saturdays 9am–5pm.

SHOPS & MARKETS

Posters

There are, at the end of the day, only two cheap ways to hide a wall, and if you don't care for paint that leaves posters. Posters also make nice souvenirs of a place, so whether it's art you want or views of Tower Bridge at sunset, the following shops are worth browsing through.

Athena, 133 Oxford Street, W1, 1 Leicester Square, WC2. Open 9.30am–6pm.

The Poster Shop, 28 James Street, WC2. Open 9.30am–6pm.

Dillon's Arts Shop, 8 Long Acre, WC2. Open 10am–6pm.

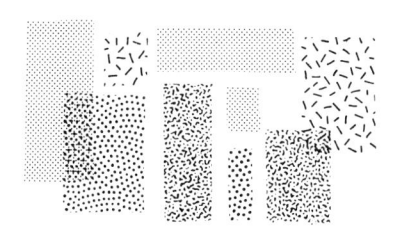

Records

The best record super-stores in London are within easy walking distance of each other in the West End. All three are seriously big, and look more like department stores than record shops. If you can't find it here, then forget it.

HMV, 363 Oxford Street, London W1. Tel: 01-629 1240. Open Mon–Sat 9.30am–6.30pm.

Tower Records, 1 Piccadilly Circus, London W1. Tel: 01-734 9915. Open Mon–Sat 10am–6pm.

Virgin Megastore, 30 Oxford Street, London W1. Tel: 01-631 1614. Open Mon–Sat 9.30am–8pm.

Smithfield Market

Not a place for vegetarians, but a wonderful experience if you'd like to watch London's huge wholesale meat market at work. Refrigerator juggernauts carrying fresh beef, lamb, pork and poultry begin arriving the night before, and by 5am the next day the entire area is in high gear. Meat is sold here by the truck or barrow load, and you can watch porters in blood-stained overalls trundling great carcasses about. Pubs and cafes in the neighbourhood are open market hours too.

Smithfield Market, London EC1. Open Mon–Fri 5am–10am.

SHOPS & MARKETS

Spitalfields Market

The City of London has had its own wholesale flower, fruit and vegetable market at Spitalfields ever since 1682. It's a huge place covering some 4.8 hectares and with stall fronts running for nearly 2 kilometres. About 1500 tonnes of fruit and vegetables are sold here daily. The flower market is tucked away to one side between Lamb and Folgate streets.

Spitalfields Market, Commercial Street, London E1. Open Mon–Sat 4.30am–10am.

Stamps

If you collect stamps a small corner of London between the Strand and Trafalgar Square is the home of a varied selection of stamp dealers. You'll find everything here from first day covers to old, rare and expensive foreign issues.

Stanley Gibbons, 399 Strand, London W2. Tel: 01-836 8444. Open Mon–Fri 9am–6pm, Sat 10am–1pm.

Stamp Mart, 79 Strand, London WC2. Tel: 01-836 2579. Open Mon–Fri 10am–5pm, Sat 10am–2pm.

London International Stamp Centre, 27 King Street, London WC2. Tel: 01-836 5871. Open Mon–Fri 10am–5pm, Sat 10am–3pm.

G.P.O. Philatelic Counters, Post Office, 24 William IV Street, London WC2. Tel: 01-930 9813. Open Mon–Sat 8am–8pm, Sun 10am–5pm.

Wembley Market

Sunday morning markets are an invention of the last 15 years or so; they make use of open areas like car parks that are empty on Sundays but in use during the rest of the week. One of the best is next to Wembley Stadium where you'll find hundreds of stalls selling cheap clothing and new household goods of every description, not to mention candy floss, doughnuts and other fairground snacks. Can be very crowded.

Wembley Market, Wembley Stadium Car Park, Middlesex. Open Sunday 9am–2pm.

Places to Eat

Taking the entire family out to eat in a restaurant isn't exactly the greatest of English traditions, but it's becoming a lot more common than it used to be. Many places now offer small portions for young kids or special children's menus, some even lay on entertainment.

Bernigra's

This restaurant has a street-service window that always seems more popular than the tables inside, but then this is where you buy Bernigra's delicious Italian ice-cream. It's the sort of place where you pick up a cone to lick as you walk down the street, window shopping all the computer and hi-fi gear along Tottenham Court Road.

Bernigra's, 69 Tottenham Court Road, London W1.

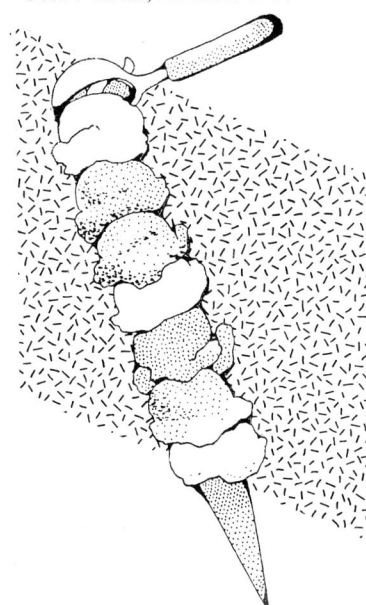

Cakes & Pastries

There are plenty of cake and coffee shops in London where you can sit down, have a snack and kill time all day long if you want – or else just drop in to pick up some pastries. These shops make delicious cakes, tarts and pastries – and serve excellent coffee as well. (See individual entries too.)

Maison Bertaux, 28 Greek Street, London W1.
Maison Bouquillon, 41 Moscow Road, London W2.
Valerie's, 44 Old Compton Street, London W1.

Deep Pan Pizza Company

The name says it all. Here is where you'll get American-style pizzas as thick as pie and served with toppings like pineapple and corn that have more in common with Iowa and Hawaii than Naples. Almost 20 restaurants in the chain from Kingston to Islington.

Deep Pan Pizza Company,

PLACES TO EAT

289 Oxford Street W1, 98 Tottenham Court Road W1, 56 Edgeware Road W2, 126 Baker Street W1, 4 Leicester Square WC2, and many more.

Dina's Diner

A small friendly caff that serves huge portions at some of the cheapest prices for meals in Covent Garden. Deserves ten Michelin stars for the quality of its chips alone, while the puddings are guaranteed to leave you staggering when you get up.

Dina's Diner, 39 Endell Street, London WC2.

Fast Food

If you can hold your breath from the time you order until the time you get your food, then you know that what you're getting is fast food. Most places have hamburgers & chips or fish & chips as a main part of the menu – either way you get the chips. Two US chains stand out. (See individual entries too.)

McDonald's, 65 branches all over London.

Wendy Restaurants, branches all over central London.

Fish & Chips

One of the big surprises an American friend of ours had as he walked the entire length of Oxford Street was that there were no fish and chip shops to be found. In fact, the centre of London, for some reason, has very few such places. Here are two of the best. (See individual entries too.)

Geales Fish Restaurant, 2 Farmer Street, London W8.

The Seashell, 51 Lisson Grove, London NW1.

Fortnum & Mason Soda Fountain

Although F&M are so grand that the staff here wear tailcoats, the Soda Fountain at the back of the shop is a great place to go for afternoon tea. A visit here comes under the heading of 'major treat' as the

PLACES TO EAT

minimum charge is £3.50.
Fortnum & Mason Soda Fountain Restaurant, 181 Piccadilly, London W1.

Garfunkel's

This chain of 21 identically-styled family restaurants has branches all around the West End. They have a wholesome American style – clean, fast, good service, reasonable prices with a separate menu just for kids – everything you'd ever want from a family restaurant in fact. And they're comfortable too.
Garfunkel's 194 Baker Street NW1, 360 Oxford Street W1, 265 Regent Street W1, 9 Kensington High Street W8.

Geales

Near Notting Hill Gate tube this restaurant is a place for sitting down to eat fish and chips. Excellent quality.
Geales Fish Restaurant, 2 Farmer Street, London W8.

Hamley's Soda Fountain

After exhausting yourself by looking at five floors of toys you can work up a real headache at the Soda Fountain, where video games accompany the ice-cream. Or take a break in the self-service restaurant, where fish, hamburgers and sandwiches – all with chips – can be had.
Hamley's, 108 Regent Street, London W1.

Harrods Ice Cream Parlour

The best known department store in Britain has a less well known ice-cream parlour on the ground floor (on the Hans Crescent side) that serves fabulous New England ice-cream, froghurt (frozen yoghurt), sundaes and really great coffee. This is rich American-style ice-cream at its best.
Harrods, Knightsbridge, London SW1.

Ice-Cream

Great ice-cream is hard to find in London – maybe that would change if there were such things as real summers – but a few

131

PLACES TO EAT

places do stand out in the crowd. (See individual entries too.)

Bernigra's, 69 Tottenham Court Road, London W1.

Harrods, Knightsbridge, London SW1.

La Maison des Sorbets, 140 Battersea Park Road, London SW11.

Marine Ices, 8 Haverstock Hill, London NW3.

La Maison des Sorbets

All the sorbet flavours you'll ever want to try, just off Battersea Park.

La Maison des Sorbets, 140 Battersea Park Road, London SW11.

Lyons Corner House

While the old one was a mess, this new-look version of the famous Corner House just off Trafalgar Square is bright, cheerful and welcoming. It's a family place, just like the original, with a coffee shop upstairs and a restaurant below. Lyons is a great location for resting your feet after the long walk up from Parliament and Downing Street, or Buckingham Palace, and serves everything from breakfast to late afternoon teas.

Lyons Corner House, 450 Strand, London WC2.

MacDonald's

At last count there were 65 MacDonald's in the London area and no doubt more have opened up since this entry was written. Day or night, you'll never be disappointed by the hamburgers you're served – they're always exactly the same as the one you had last time. The french fries are worth a visit themselves. The child has yet to be born who doesn't like eating at MacDonald's.

MacDonald's, 65 Shaftesbury Avenue W1, 35 Strand WC2, 310 Regent Street W1, 8–10 Oxford Street W1, 108 Kensington High Street W8, and many others.

Magic Moments

Here is a fast-food restaurant in Regent Street which you enter by walking through a picture.

The place is best known for the magician who wanders about doing tricks at customers' tables (making food vanish isn't one of them).
The Magic Moments Restaurant, 233 Regent Street, London W1.

Maison Bertaux

Choose your cakes downstairs then go up to find a table. Right in the heart of Soho just north of Shaftesbury Avenue.
Maison Bertaux, 28 Greek Street, London W1.

Maison Bouquillon

Near Bayswater tube station this pastry shop is well worth a detour if you've been walking in Hyde Park; in fact it's a good reason for pretending to go for a walk in the first place. What they can do with chocolate is enough to make strong men weep.
Maison Bouquillon, 41 Moscow Road, London W2.

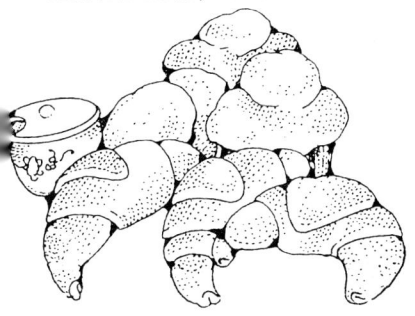

Marine Ices

For the past two million years people in north London have been inventing excuses to visit Chalk Farm to eat ice cream here. The front of the shop sells only delicious Italian ice-cream, the back is a small Italian restaurant. But it's the dozens of ice-creams, sorbets and cassatta that draw people back again and again. The shop's name comes from the design of the place which is supposed to be a ship – of sorts.
Marine Ices, 8 Haverstock Hill, London NW3.

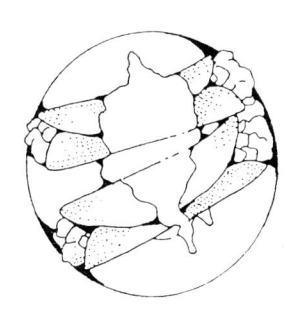

My Old Dutch

Huge pancakes with 67 different types of fillings make this a terrific place to astound a kid. The pancakes are thin so even the biggest are no problem to finish. A great novelty.
My Old Dutch, 131 High Holborn, London WC1.

PLACES TO EAT

Pappagalli's Pizza

A theme pizza and pasta restaurant that does children's portions and can provide colouring books and crayons to keep them happy if the food isn't enough.

Pappagalli's Pizza, 7–9 Swallow Street, London W1.

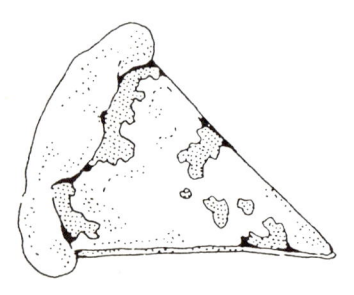

Performing Meals

Some restaurants will do almost anything to take your mind off the food you're eating. Usually this takes the form of 'in-flight' entertainment along the lines of magicians and other performers. (See individual entries too.)

Magic Moments Restaurant, 233 Regent Street, London W1.

Smollensky's Balloon, 1 Dover Street, London W1.

The Satellite Cafe, 8 Argyll Street, London W1.

Pizza

Like mushrooms after the rain, pizza restaurants have cropped up by the dozen in recent years. They're always good value, have quick service, and the best are all worth second and third visits. (See individual entries too.)

Deep Pan Pizza Company, all over central London.

Pappagalli's Pizza, 7–9 Swallow Street, London W1.

Pizza Express, branches all round London.

Pizza Pasta Factory, The Trocadero, 7 Rupert Street, London W1.

Pizza Express

London's original and, to many people's way of thinking, best pizza chain, now with 19 outlets. They only do thin, Italian-style pizzas, not the deep-dish American versions that have become popular in recent years. Branches all around London.

Pizza Express, 11 Knightsbridge SW1, 10 Dean Street W1, 29 Wardour Street W1, 30 Coptic Street WC1, and many more.

Pizza Pasta Factory

Right off Piccadilly Circus in the Trocadero Centre is an Italian piazza where you can sit at 'outdoor tables' and have pizzas, fresh pasta and desserts. The restaurant is busy, but never packed, and a really useful place to stop after you've visited the Guinness World of Records upstairs.

Mario & Franco's Pizza Pasta Factory, The Trocadero, 7 Rupert Street, London W1.

Porters

There's something about pies that make them great kid's food – it may have to do with finding an entire meal under a single piecrust roof. Porters specializes in the traditional English kinds with lamb, chicken, fish and vegetable fillings, while their puddings are the real thing from school days – treacle tart, bread and butter pudding, steamed syrup sponges and spotted dick. Lip-smacking stuff, to be sure.

Porters, 17 Henrietta Street, Covent Garden, London WC2.

Selfridges Basement & Top of the Shop

Exhaustion on Oxford Street is an occupational hazard for any visitor to London. Two comfortable places where you can collapse are the Basement Bistro and the Top of the Shop restaurants at Selfridges Department Store. The Basement Bistro is a self-service counter while Top of the Shop does really cheap portions of fish fingers and sausages and other great kids' food.

Selfridges, Oxford Street, London W1.

Smollensky's Balloon

A normal enough sort of place (near Green Park) during the week with a children's menu of pasta and burgers, but on Sunday's you can have brunch here from noon while a magician performs or a Punch & Judy show is staged.

Smollensky's Balloon, 1 Dover Street, London W1.

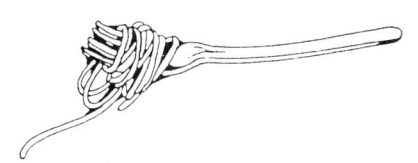

Texas Lone Star Saloon

Tex-Mex food has undergone a minor boom (okay – boomlet) in London in the last few years. Any kid who'd love to eat in a western saloon will go for this place in a big way. You'll get American food along the lines of spare ribs, guacamole ('gwack-a-moley') dip, tacos and other Mexican dishes that are hot even when they're cold, and of course pecan pie.

Texas Lone Star Saloon, 154 Gloucester Road, London SW7, 117 Queensway, London W2.

PLACES TO EAT

The L.A. Café

More Californian and Mexican food with special menus for kids. Between 6 and 7 o'clock, children can create their own custom-made pizzas.

The L.A. Café, 163 Knightsbridge, London SW7.

The Satellite Café

Almost as much a zoo as the one in Regent's Park – but without the animals – here you can have the experience of watching yourself eat on video (this place used to be known as The Video Cafe) while you eat at the table (an entirely new twist to the idea of TV dinners!). Floor-to-ceiling banks of video monitors play cartoons and rock videos, and make you forget that what you're eating is hamburgers and fries.

The Satellite Café, 8 Argyll Street (near Oxford Circus tube), London W1.

The Seashell

Said to be the best fish and chip shop in London (we agree!), and if you judge it by the length of the queues and the line of taxis parked outside you'll have to, too. This restaurant is a bit outside the centre of town but well worth the trip.

The Seashell of Lisson Grove, Lisson Grove, London NW1.

Valerie's

A landmark in Soho is Patisserie Valerie, home for much of the film and publishing industry, and anyone else who can bag an empty seat. Popular is an understatement for this place.

Patisserie Valerie, 44 Old Compton Street, London W1.

Wendy Restaurants

Straight competition to MacDonald's, with slightly better burgers according to some kids we know. Others would argue.

Wendy Restaurants, 24 Haymarket W1, 79 Oxford Street W1, Cambridge Circus WC2, 57 Strand WC2.

Entertainment

There are four parts to this section; shows & plays, music & concerts, films, and free entertainment. Within each part entries are listed alphabetically.

Shows & Plays: Many of the theatres and arts centres that have regular seasons of childrens' performances are outside the West End. Aside from producing plays and family shows, they also have workshops, puppet shows, mime, clowns and juggling, films, and other family events; most performances are staged on weekends and holidays. Phone for details of what's on, prices and times before you go along.

Albany Empire

This theatre in south London has performances for kids on the last Saturday of each month.
  Albany Empire, Douglas Way, Deptford, London E8. Tel: 01-691 8016.

Croydon Warehouse Theatre

Saturday mornings, switch off the TV and go along to the puppet shows, mime, juggling, clowning and other events that are held here for kids of all ages.
  Croydon Warehouse Theatre, 62 Dingwall Road, Croydon, Surrey. Tel: 01-680 4060.

Battersea Arts Centre

On Sunday afternoons there are weekly family shows that may include plays, mime, clowns, dance or puppets. There's also a puppet centre here with a small exhibition of puppets.
  Battersea Arts Centre, Old Town Hall, Lavender Hill, London SW11. Tel: 01-223 8413.

Lauderdale Arts Centre

Regular Saturday morning shows for all the family are staged here – mime, puppets, juggling and magic – in north London.
  Lauderdale Community Arts Centre, Lauderdale House, Waterlow Park, Highgate Hill, London N6. Tel: 01-348 8716.

ENTERTAINMENT

Little Angel Marionette

A wonderful little puppet theatre that's been running for over 20 years and which stages a huge range of shows, both by a resident company and by visiting puppet troupes from all around the world. Saturday mornings there is almost always something for kid's aged three to five years; shows for older ages are scheduled for the afternoon.
Little Angel Marionette Theatre, 14 Dagmar Passage, Cross Street, London N1. Tel: 01-226 1787.

Lyric Theatre

Most Saturday mornings at 11am there are special children's events – plays, clowns, puppets, storytelling – followed by lunch in the theatre.
Lyric Theatre, King Street, Hammersmith, London W6. Tel: 01-741 2311.

Molecule Theatre of Science

This company is based at the Bloomsbury Theatre, but also tours widely around the country. The idea behind its ingenious performances is to stage adventure plays with a scientific theme. Younger audiences get the science wrapped in classic showbiz fun with plots, characters, stage fights and songs. For older kids over 13 there are also weekend talks with lively lectures by well-respected scientists (*Why is the Earth Like Porridge?* was the title of one).
Molecule Theatre of Science, Bloomsbury Theatre, 15 Gordon Street, London WC1. Tel: 01-387 9629.

National Theatre

More things to do here than you can shake a stick at with story-telling, puppet shows, workshops, clowns; most of it held during summer school holidays and at Christmas.
National Theatre, South Bank, London SE1. Tel: 01-633 0880.

Orange Tree Theatre

During the spring half-term holiday late in May, and in the summer there are regular performances for children aged three to eight years.

Orange Tree Theatre, 45 Kew Road, Richmond, Surrey. Tel: 01-940 3633.

Polka Children's Theatre

One of the best kid's theatres anywhere, everything that is staged here is for the benefit of children up to 12 years. The shows are specially commissioned and range widely – with mime, magic, music, dance, drama, puppets and humans in the same show. Some performances make use of ultra-violet light or shadow puppetry from the Far East.

Tours behind the scenes of this 300-seat theatre can also be arranged. The theatre complex is worth a visit itself. It includes an adventure room, a display of hand-made British toys and of puppets from around the world, workshops where kids can build their own puppets, a café where the food comes around on little trains, and a playground.

Polka Children's Theatre, 240 The Broadway, Wimbledon, London SW19. Tel: 01-543 4888.

Puppet Theatre Barge

From October to April every year a converted Thames barge moored at Camden Lock becomes the floating home for puppet shows on weekends – also during half term and other school holidays.

Puppet Theatre Barge, Camden Lock, London NW1. Tel: 01-249 6876.

Riverside Studios

Regular children's shows – plays, puppets, clowns – every Saturday afternoon at 12.30pm which last about an hour. Afterwards you can have lunch at the self-service restaurant here. There are family shows and pantomimes at Christmas.

Riverside Studios, Crisp Road, Hammersmith, London W6. Tel: 01-748 3354.

ENTERTAINMENT

Sadler's Wells Theatre

In the autumn the Whirligig company and other troupes stage children's performances here, and also at Christmas.
Sadler's Wells Theatre, Rosebery Avenue, London EC1. Tel: 01-278 6563.

St Georges Theatre

Shows featuring poetry, music, mime, clowns and plays for kids aged three to 12 years old on Saturday afternoons during the winter. During holidays there are workshops in acting, set-painting, prop-making, make-up, mask and puppet construction and other aspects of the theatre.
St Georges Theatre, 49 Tufnell Park Road, London N7. Tel: 01-607 1128.

Tricycle Theatre

There are regular, and usually excellent theatrical performances for children on Saturdays at 11.30am and also during half term and other school holidays. After school hours there are workshops for children over six years with story-telling, mime and improvised acting.
Tricycle Theatre, 269 Kilburn High Road, London NW6. Tel: 01-328 8626.

Unicorn Theatre for Children

Throughout the year there are regular productions of plays, cabaret, musicals, magic shows and puppets for children aged four to 12 years. The Unicorn Club organizes workshops on weekends and school holidays.
Unicorn Theatre for Children, Arts Theatre, 6 Great Newport Street, London WC2. Tel: 01-836 3334.

Watermans Arts Centre

On weekends there are regular story-telling events or clown and puppet shows, while at Christmas and in summer children's plays are staged.

Watermans Arts Centre, 40 High Street, Brentford, Middlesex. Tel: 01-847 5651.

Whirligig Theatre

Although this is a touring company, when it's in London you can see some of their wonderful dramatic and musical productions that have been specially written and produced for school-age children. They tour with one new play a year, performing always in different theatres. Phone to find out where Whirligig is currently appearing.
Whirligig Theatre, Tel: 01-947 1732.

Young Vic

There is a regular season of plays and musicals for young people with matinees on Saturday afternoons.
Young Vic Theatre, 66 The Cut, London SE1. Tel: 01-928 6363.

Music & Concerts: There are lots of places in London where you can listen to live music that is especially suited to children; the venues range from crowded Tube stations to concert halls and cathedrals.

Buskers

People playing guitars, violins, saxophones and other musical instruments can often be heard in Tube stations. Here they stake out a pitch and play for money; usually there's a hat or box to collect the coins passers-by throw their way. While London Transport doesn't exactly encourage buskers it generally seems to tolerate them. One thing for sure they certainly make commuting a lot more pleasurable.

However, at the Piazza, Covent Garden, buskers are positively welcomed by the management and, as a result, have become a big tourist attraction.

Musical routines usually take up a pitch under a covered area at one end of the market. Street theatre acts are at the opposite end in front of St Paul's Church. The standard of both is high – and is kept that way by the market authorities who audition the buskers before they can perform in public.
Covent Garden Market, London WC2.

ENTERTAINMENT

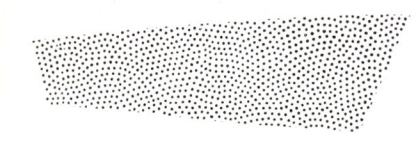

City Music

Throughout the City of London, at lunchtime, a number of churches hold concerts – chamber music, organ recitals and recordings in the main – that are intended for people on their lunch break. Go along with the regulars if you want to enjoy some free entertainment in an unusual setting. There are usually posters outside the churches announcing what's on. The following have regular programmes:

St Botolph without Bishopsgate, EC2, St Olave's, Hart Street, EC3, St Stephen Walbrook, Walbrook EC4, All Hallows-by-the-Tower, Byward Street EC3, St Bartholomew-the-Great, Smithfield EC1, St Mary-le-Bow, Cheapside EC2, Southwark Cathedral, Cathedral Street SE1.

Concerts for Children – I

Every winter between October and May there are six concerts for children over seven years old held on Saturdays at the Royal Festival Hall on the South Bank. The approach to the music is light-hearted with the conductors pointing out instruments and the sound effects they can make. Each concert starts with an audience song rehearsal.

You can get tickets from the promoters at 01-870 1655 or obtain a brochure directly from:

Ernest Read Music Association, 9 Cotsford Avenue, New Malden, Surrey. Tel: 01-942 0318.

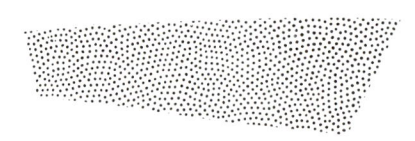

Concerts for Children – II

There is another series of autumn and winter concerts that introduce children to classical music and which are held on Saturday mornings at Fairfield Hall in Croydon.

Arthur Davison Orchestral Concerts, Fairfield Hall, Croydon. Tel: 01-688 9291.

Concerts for Children – III

The BBC sponsors a series of six concerts for eight to 13 year-olds every year at the Royal Festival Hall. The concerts are on Saturday mornings between October and March and the music ranges from the 1700s to the present.

Robert Mayer Concerts for Children, Royal Festival Hall, South Bank, London SE1. For tickets phone the BBC at: 01-927 4523.

Fun with Music

Around Christmas every year Ann Rachlin gives a series of concerts at the Barbican with the London Concert Orchestra. These are specially aimed to introduce children to classical music by telling them stories about the private lives of famous classical composers.

Barbican Centre, Silk Street, London EC2. Tel: 01-628 8795.

Morley College Family Concerts

This series of six relaxed concerts held at Morley College on Saturday mornings, one a month from October to March, introduces parents and children to a wide range of music including Broadway show music, classical, electronic, pop music and much else.

Morley College Family Concerts, 61 Westminster Bridge Road, London SE1. Tel: 01-928 8501.

Royal Festival Hall

At various times throughout the year music performances, dance and concerts for children are held here. The programme can include story-telling and singing.

Royal Festival Hall, South Bank, London SE1. Tel: 01-928 3191.

Films: London has so many cinemas and film clubs that you'll never run out of places to go. Quite a number of them run special showings of kids' films on Saturdays, or else have seasons of children's films at various times of the year.

Barbican Children's Cinema

In the Barbican Centre on Saturdays there are two performances of children's films for six to 12 year-olds (one at 11am and one at 2.30pm). You pay an annual membership fee of £1.00 to join the Children's Cinema Club and from then on can go to see any film for just £1.00 a visit. The films change weekly.

Barbican Cinema Club, Barbican Centre, Silk Street, London EC2. Tel: 01-628 8795.

Battersea Arts Centre

Films for children are shown on Saturday and Sunday afternoons at 3.30pm. Phone beforehand to find out what's on the programme.

Battersea Arts Centre, Old Town Hall, Lavender Hill, London SW11. Tel: 01-223 6557.

ICA Children's Cinema Club

This is the kind of club everyone should join – mainly because it's free with the first cinema ticket you buy. Once you're in you get a membership card and a monthly newsletter of what's on. On Saturday and Sunday afternoons, among a wide range of offerings, there are animated films, Bob Hope-Bing Crosby movies and other comedies, also musicals, serials and much more. The ICA has a great self-service cafe too, in case sitting in the dark in front of a screen for a couple of hours makes you hungry.

ICA, Nash House, 12 Carlton House Terrace, The Mall, London SW1. Tel: 01-930 3647.

National Film Theatre

On weekend afternoons an enormous range of movies gets shown in the Junior NFT (for kids under 16), often with

special series of films based on a theme – adventure, pirates, animation and so forth. Comedies, cartoons, science fiction, old and new films all get screened here. When you join the Junior NFT you also get a badge and poster to colour. Sometimes there are talks on how films are made or even workshops on making movies. There is a good restaurant and snack bar in the cinema complex, and with the Thames nearby it's easy to spend hours here without ever getting bored.
NFT, South Bank, London SE1. Tel: 01-928 3232.

Saturday Morning Cinema Club

Main cinemas very often run Saturday morning clubs that show children's films at cheap prices. To find out what's on check with local newspapers or ring the cinema itself.

Screen on the Hill

There is a Saturday Kids Club at this modern cinema in north London that presents films and live entertainment every weekend at 10.30am. You need to be a member to take in the show.
Screen on the Hill, 199 Haverstock Hill, London NW3. Tel: 01-435 3366.

Special Cinemas

On weekends some London museums show special films linked to the subjects they have on display. The films are entertaining as well as informative. For example, the Imperial War Museum might screen old newsreels or training films from World War II used to welcome US troops to Britain, or to teach sailors how to survive in open lifeboats after being torpedoed. In all cases the shows are free.
The Geological Museum, Exhibition Road, London SW7. Tel: 01-589 3444. Saturdays at 2.30pm.
Imperial War Museum, Lambeth Road, London SE1. Tel: 01-735 8922. Saturdays & Sundays in the afternoon.
Science Museum, Exhibition Road, London SW7. Tel: 01-589 3456. Saturdays at 12.30pm.

ENTERTAINMENT

Free Entertainment: The great thing about free entertainment is the price; the downside is that you can't complain if you don't like what you get. But if you're looking for ways to spend time without spending money, there's always plenty to choose from. Here are a few ideas.

Barbican Centre

In August every year there is a big Family Festival, with lots happening for children less than 12 years old. There are concerts by the London Symphony Orchestra, model-making competitions, children's stories in the library, chess tournaments, films, workshops – lots of them free. Well worth getting a programme beforehand to find out what's happening.

Barbican Centre, Silk Street, London EC2. Tel: 01-638 4141 (ask for information).

National Theatre Family Events

During the summer school holidays there are all kinds of activities for children and adults along the South Bank here. Buskers, street theatre and local pop groups give performances. There are workshops in puppet-making, clowns and mime artists perform, jugglers juggle, and storytellers read from their books. There are also plays specially for young audiences. Lots of events are free.

National Theatre, South Bank, London SE1. Tel: 01-633 0880.

Open Air Art

If you need an excuse to take a walk but don't have a dog, then head for two of the world's longest galleries (where you can wander for hours if the weather's good) and take in the arts and crafts and the fresh air at one and the same time. The 'art' may be suspect, as is the 'fresh air' (because of the traffic), but it's a great way to look at paintings, sculpture and odd sorts of craftwork.

ENTERTAINMENT

Everything's for sale in case you're hunting for souvenirs.

Green Park, railings along Piccadilly, Saturdays & Sundays.

Hyde Park, railings along Bayswater Road, Sundays.

Punch and Judy

Back in 1662, the first ever Punch and Judy show was performed outside St Paul's Church, Covent Garden by an Italian showman, Silvio Fiorillo, who brought his collection of motley glove puppets to England and soon found he had a rave success on his hands. The fool in his performances, a particularly violent character called Punchinello, eventually stole the show and along the way took on the English name of Punch. Soon after, he was joined by a wife, Judy, and a dog, while a whole raft of other characters – like a policeman with a truncheon – were added over the years.

Early in May there is a Punch and Judy Festival in the grounds of St Paul's Church, while in October another one is held in Covent Garden Piazza. The rest of the year, most weekends, there are regular shows beside St Paul's Church on the west side of the market.

Punch & Judy Show, Covent Garden Piazza, Sat–Sun 11am–4pm (shows on the hour, early spring to late autumn).

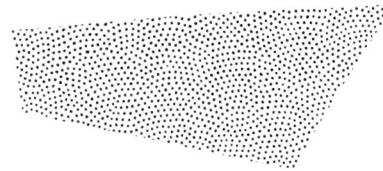

Speakers' Corner

For over 100 years this small patch of Hyde Park has been a place of unfettered free speech. Speakers get up on boxes and talk to (or 'at') the public about anything under the sun; religion and politics usually guarantee a good crowd, but almost any topic may come up. Weekend afternoons are the busiest and best times to catch this free show.

Gardens, Parks & Walks

London has something like 800 public parks and gardens, including six Royal Parks, with more green space than any other capital city in Europe. These areas range from pocket-sized patches (King George VI Park in Wandsworth) to huge, half-wild expanses (Richmond Park is over 1000 hectares) with enough in them to take a lifetime to explore.

If you don't live in Britain you might find it odd that many parks are locked up at night – the tradition is to shut the gates at dusk – since the English treat their public parks like private property. As there's no chance of a park escaping, it's a habit that probably has something to do with loving walls and fences.

Alexandra Palace & Park

The park slopes steeply around the massive bulk of Alexandra Palace – now being rebuilt after a disastrous fire a few years ago. The best thing here is the view over much of north London. There is also a little boating lake, a pitch-and-putt golf course, a practice ski-slope (no snow, but a plastic run that's good all year round) and a children's adventure playground. Funfairs come to the park on Bank Holiday weekends and there are often special fairs and exhibitions inside the 'temporary' Pavilion building.

Alexandra Palace & Park, Muswell Hill, London N22. Open daily, 24 hours.

Battersea Park

Right next to the squat bulk of the now-defunct Battersea Power Station, and running along the south bank of the Thames, Battersea Park has something for everyone. There's a summertime children's zoo with peacocks, deer, ducks, geese and pony rides; there's a big boating lake, a flower garden with a fountain in the shape of a Viking ship, and also

GARDENS & PARKS

tennis courts and a running track for joggers. On the river side there's a path where you can stroll and look across to Chelsea.

At Easter there's a colourful, mile-long parade around the outside of the park on the Sunday, with brightly-coloured floats and bands.

Battersea Park, Queenstown Road, London SW11. Open daily to dusk.

Blackheath

The most noticeable difference between commons and parks is that the former are unfenced. It's a relic from the Middle Ages when commons were village wasteland that could be used by everyone.

Blackheath Common, in southeast London, butts up to Greenwich Park on one side and spreads toward the village of Blackheath on the other. It's a large open expanse, almost treeless, and so attracts lots of kite-flyers, footballers and dog-walkers (though the dogs seem to miss the trees).

This common is where James I introduced golf to the British in 1608 (though there is no course here to mark that great historical event), and where Watt Tyler camped his peasant army in 1381.

Blackheath, London SE3. Open daily, 24 hours.

Bushey Park

A less well-known park which surrounds Hampton Court Palace on two sides and which also borders the Thames, it covers more than 400 hectares and is a great place for a picnic in summer – you can combine lunch with a visit to Hampton Court Palace. There is a herd of tame deer in the park and a flock of sheep that, between them, do most of the gardening.

Bushey Park, Hampton, Middlesex. Open daily, 6.30am–midnight.

Chelsea Physic Garden

A physic garden is not somewhere to go to get physical but is an old term for a botanical garden. Although this garden was established in 1673, and is a genuine antique in it's own right (it is also the second

GARDENS & PARKS

oldest botanic garden in the country), it was only recently opened to the public. Here, in a crowded 1.6-hectare plot, you can take a look at some 5000 species of plants, trees and medicinal and culinary herbs. The Physic Garden shop sells plants, cards and guidebooks.

Chelsea Physic Garden, 66 Royal Hospital Road (entrance in Swan Walk), London SW3. Tel: 01-352 5646. Open April–Oct, Sun and Wed afternoons only. Admission adults £1.50, children £1.00.

Crystal Palace Park

This south London park and sports centre is home to more huffing and puffing than almost anywhere else in London. You can find everything here from skiing on an artificial slope to pounding along a cross-country running track, although you might prefer the quiet of the boating lake.

The islands in the lake are something special; here, half-hidden by the undergrowth, are 20 life-size (though often inaccurate) models of dinosaurs that were made for the Great Exhibition of 1851. Elsewhere in the park there's a children's zoo, and in July and August open-air Sunday evening concerts are held in the Concert Bowl.

Crystal Palace Park, Norwood, London SE19. Open daily, dawn to dusk.

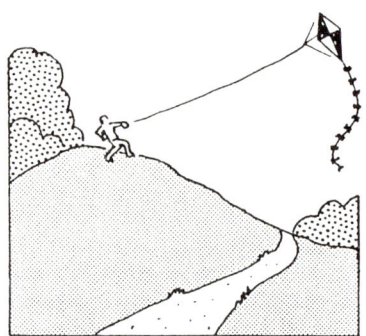

Hampstead Heath

Here in one of London's wilder and hillier parks you can explore 320 hectares of woodland, ponds and fields. It's a great place for a picnic and a day of wandering about in north London.

There are twelve ponds on the Heath, three of which are set aside for fishing and three for swimming; dogs and ducks make the most use of the others. From the top of Parliament Hill at the southern end of the Heath there are great views across the centre of London, all the way to Crystal Palace and beyond. The hill is also a favourite place for flying kites, while at the foot of it there's an adventure

GARDENS & PARKS

playground and a paddling pool for kids.

At the north end of the Heath is Kenwood House, a stately home where, on summer evenings, open-air concerts are held on a shell-like bandstand overlooking a small lake.

On Bank Holiday weekends funfairs move onto the Heath and set up with big-wheels, rides and dozens of stalls.

Hampstead Heath, London NW3. Open daily, 24 hours.

Hampton Court Gardens

Aside from the palace at Hampton Court, there are also wonderful gardens and a deer park here; they are free – unlike the palace. You'll find beautiful walled gardens, an ancient vine said to have roots that reach a mind-boggling distance to the Thames, old yew trees and tennis courts built during the reign of Henry VIII.

The shrubbery maze at Hampton Court is world famous – there's a small charge to go in – and if you want to find out how easy it is to get lost give it a test.

Hampton Court Gardens, Hampton Court Road, East Molesey, Surrey. Open daily, 7am–hour before dusk.

Holland Park

This beautiful park to the west of Kensington was once the private grounds of Holland House. Younger kids will like the walk through the woods where there are half-tame rabbits, ducks and peacocks. Among the park's many attractions are its walks, playing fields, a play area for children, a summertime open-air theatre and a Dutch Garden famous for tulips. There are also snack bars and a very good restaurant here.

Holland Park, High Street Kensington, London W8. Open daily, 8am–dusk.

Hyde Park

The most famous Royal Park in London consists of 144 hectares of greenery, stretching from Park Lane west to Notting Hill Gate, and from Bayswater

GARDENS & PARKS

south to Knightsbridge.

In the middle is the Serpentine, a lake where you can row boats and canoes, feed the ducks, fish or go for a swim in the roped off area known as the Lido. There's also a paddling pool here and a sandpit for young children. A restaurant and snack bar overlook the lake.

At the southern end of the park you'll sometimes see people, or soldiers from nearby Hyde Park Barracks, riding horses along a dirt track known as Rotten Row – an odd name for what is one of the most fashionable parts of London. Actually it's just the way we English torture the French for 'King's Road' – *Route du Roi*.

If you're in the park on the day of a royal birthday, chances are you'll hear an artillery gun salute being fired.

Hyde Park, London W1. Open daily, dawn–midnight.

Kensington Gardens

This is a large park which runs alongside Hyde Park on the west side. Originally it was part of the hunting grounds used by Henry VIII.

At one end is Kensington Palace, part of which is open to the public (the rest of it is still lived in by members of the Royal Family). Elsewhere there are especially beautiful flower displays along Flower Walk (near to the Albert Memorial) and in the Sunken Garden, while the mini-lake called Round Pond is often used for sailing model ships. Close to Hyde Park, by the lake known as Long Water, there's a famous statue of Peter Pan that commemorates his creator, the author J. M. Barrie. There is also a pet cemetery tucked away in another corner of the park.

Kensington Gardens, London W2. Open daily, 7.30am–dusk.

Kew Gardens

Though its correct name is the Royal Botanic Gardens, most Londoners know this place as Kew Gardens.

Along with Hampstead Heath it's one of the best places in London for a lazy picnic, with more than 120 hectares of woodlands, gardens and ponds to choose from and more than 50,000 different kinds of plants to talk to.

GARDENS & PARKS

Some of the most spectacular parts of Kew Gardens are the glasshouses. There's a Palm House where you'll find palms from all around the world, a Succulent House full of cacti, and a sauna-like Tropical Waterlily House where giant water lilies with leaves 2 metres across grow in ponds. The small Wood Museum has examples of all kinds of British timber and there's also a museum of useful plants that includes tea, coffee, cocoa, medicinal herbs, poisons, rubber and lots of less well-known species that we regularly make use of. What an education!

Kew Gardens, Kew, Surrey. Open daily, 10am–dusk. Admission adults £0.50, children under 10 are free.

Regent's Park

This Royal Park just to the north of Madame Tussaud's and the Planetarium is also the home of London Zoo; you can see the wolf enclosure as you go along Broad Walk. Running past the zoo around the top of the park is the Regent's Canal with a towpath you can walk along.

Aside from playing fields, tennis courts, and children's playgrounds there is also a boating pond for children that's open in the summer and a famous open-air theatre running from June to August that only stages productions of Shakespeare plays. Nearby in the Inner Circle is a beautiful rose garden (especially in June) and, more importantly, there's also a good snack bar/restaurant near here.

Regent's Park, London NW1. Open daily, dawn–dusk.

Richmond Park

It's wild, it has herds of deer and it's easy to get lost in, and at 1000 hectares Richmond Park is by far the biggest open space in London. You can walk for hours here without ever re-crossing your path (or finding your way out!).

In 1637, Charles I enclosed this park, which was a royal hunting reserve, and its herds of red and fallow deer have been wandering about freely here ever since. One hilly part, called Isabella Plantation, is an enclosed woodland garden full of azaleas and magnolias.

If you're feeling active you can ride, play football or cricket, or fish in the large ponds here.

Richmond Park, Richmond, Surrey. Open daily, 7am–dusk.

Royal Botanic Gardens (See Kew Gardens)

GARDENS & PARKS

St James's Park

Certainly a contender for the title of 'London's Prettiest Park' St James's is tucked away between Whitehall and Buckingham Palace and features in half the spy movies set in London; it's here that grey-suited bureaucrats meet on the bridge over the lake to feed pigeons and ducks and discuss spy business. But you don't have to be a civil servant to come here to enjoy the view of Whitehall and the Palace, or to admire the flower beds and the pelicans which live in a small sanctuary at one end of the park. An aptly named Cake House serves tea and other refreshments.

St James's Park, The Mall, London SW1. Open daily, dawn–dusk.

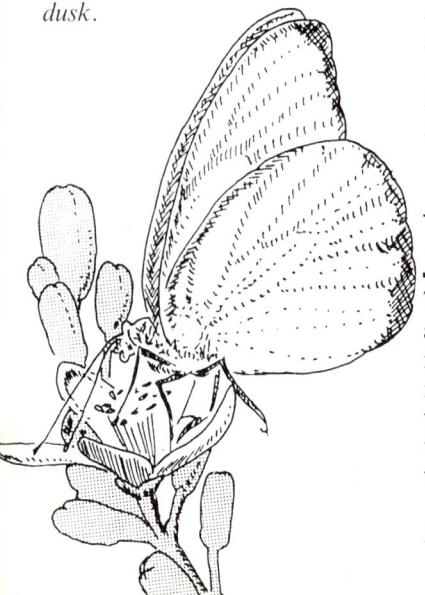

Syon Park

This 22-hectare riverside park is just across the Thames from Kew Gardens. It's a great place to bring kids, if not for the 6-acre rose garden or the conservatory with an aviary and aquarium inside, then for the Butterfly House (with free-flying butterflies) and the British Motor Industry Heritage Museum, where the history of British cars is displayed with 100 models from 1895. Or else you can visit Syon House, the magnificent London home of the Duke of Northumberland. There's also a cafeteria and a restaurant.

Syon Park, Brentford, Middlesex. Open April–Oct 10am–5pm, Nov–Mar 10am–3.30pm. Admission £0.75 adults, £0.60 children; Park and House £1.50 adults, £1.00 children; Motor Museum £1.75 adults, £1.00 children; Butterfly House £1.90 adults, £1.10 children.

Trent Park

This 160-hectare country park at the end of the Piccadilly Line is the place to go if you want to ride horses, fish, golf or go for a walk along one of the nature trails here. There's also a small working farm that you can visit.

Trent Park, Cockfosters, Barnet. Open daily, 24 hours.

GARDENS & PARKS

Views

London is, for the most part, a low, flat city. There are no steep hills with spectacular lookouts in the middle of it, and 70-storey skyscrapers with visitors galleries are unheard of. If you want a bird's eye view the following places are some of the best:

Hampstead Heath at Parliament Hill or across the road from Whitestone Pond.

St Paul's Cathedral offers one of the best views over central London. From the high gallery at the top of the dome you can see across the City or past Fleet Street to the West End.

The Monument, at 60 metres, is just high enough to give you a view around parts of the City and the Thames. It's a 311-step climb to the top so you might want to train a bit before you tackle it.

Tower Bridge has a high-level walkway with views along the river and over the Tower of London.

Westminster Cathedral has an 85-metre tower (go up by lift or stairs) from which you can look over nearby Victoria Station and take in views from Buckingham Palace to the Houses of Parliament.

Walks

There are a few sign-posted walks around London that let you explore the city at your own pace. They're all free, and you come back healthier than when you set out.

Guided Walks: Various organisations run guided tours on foot around London. Their guides are both knowledgeable and good on local colour. You'll probably end up knowing a lot more about London than any of the natives do. Most tours start from the ticket offices of tube stations at pre-arranged times.

London Walks have a dozen or so walks that range from Jack the Ripper's London to tours of Legal London.

London Walks, 139 Conway Street, N14. Tel: 01-882 2763.

Streets of London do 12 different tours of up to two hours in length (Haunted London, Lawyer's London, City in the Blitz).

Streets of London, 32 Grovelands Road, London N13. Tel: 01-882 3414.

GARDENS & PARKS

Middle Thames: Along the north bank of the river between Barnes Bridge and Hammersmith Bridge is a riverside walk that runs past lawned terraces (great for views of the Oxford and Cambridge Boat Race) and, after a short detour through a small housing estate, continues past lines of beautiful houses and riverside pubs (in one, *The Dove*, James Thompson wrote *Rule Britannia*). Starts Barnes Bridge British Rail station, ends Hammersmith tube station.

Silver Jubilee Walk: This walking path of almost 9 kilometres opened in 1977 on the Queen's Jubilee. It runs from Leicester Square to the Tower of London through many of the oldest parts of London. Jubilee crowns set into the pavement mark the way, or else get a guide to the route from the London Visitor & Convention Bureau at Victoria Station. They also do a booklet called *A Walk Through Spitalfields*; this slightly spooky part of the East End is fascinating to explore.

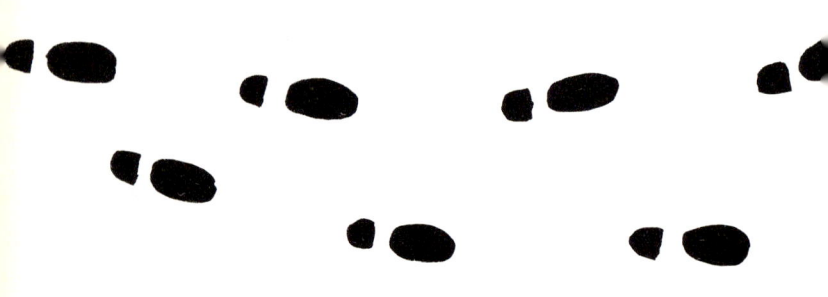

Parkland Walk: This disused train line has had the tracks removed and been turned into a ribbon of green that runs about 6 kilometres from Finsbury Park to Alexandra Park in north London. Start at Finsbury Park tube station, end at Highgate tube station.

Upper Thames: The Thames between Richmond and Kingston is only as wide as a big canal as it passes through some of the prettiest suburbs in London. A walk along the riverbank here takes you through scenic meadows and fields. Start at Richmond tube station, end at Kingston British Rail station.

Waterways

There are only two waterways of note in London (if you don't count boating ponds) – the river and the canal. On the Thames you can chug upstream as far as Hampton Court, or float down river all the way to the flood barrier at Woolwich. While the Regent's Canal meanders right across north London you can only cruise along it for a short distance, although this does take you through the most scenic parts.

Boats to Hire

If you're brave, or have some Viking blood still floating in your veins, you can hire rowing boats and canoes in various public parks in London and go raiding around the shores of a boating pond.

Parks with boating lakes: Alexandra Palace Park; Battersea Park; Crystal Palace Park; Hyde Park; Regent's Park.

Canal Trips

London is served by two major canals – the Regent's and the Grand Union; the former connects with the Thames at Limehouse, the latter at Brentford. At several locations along the way you can join canal cruises, some of them in traditional brightly-painted narrow boats; the big advantage here is that nobody ever seems to get canal-sick.

Jason's Trip: A short cruise from Little Venice to Camden Lock through Regent's Park, the trip each way takes 45 minutes. The service runs twice a day, Easter to October. Tel: 01-286 3428 for price and time details.

Jenny Wren: A sightseeing canal ride that last 90 minutes for the round trip and which runs from Camden Lock to

Little Venice. The service operates from Easter to September. Jenny Wren also do a restaurant cruise along the same route (so that's where the ducks have gone!). Tel: 01-485 4433 for times and price details.

London Waterbus: A really different way to visit London Zoo is with the London Waterbus, which starts from Little Venice. The trip lasts 30 minutes, and a ticket bought on the boat also gives you free admission to the Zoo. Runs from April to October.

London Waterbus also do a day-long trip from Camden Lock all the way to Limehouse, where there is an hour's break, and then back via a slightly different route. Tel: 01-482 2550 for times and prices.

Canal Walks

The Regent's Canal runs from Southall in west London all the way to Limehouse, near the Isle of Dogs, in the east. For much of the time it threads its way through dreary industrial settings, yet there are long stretches which are perfect for walking – or slow canal cruising.

The canal towpath was originally built for the horses which hauled barges, and continued to do so right up to the 1950s.

The path from Little Venice to Limehouse, for example, runs for 14 kilometres, and along the way passes some of the prettiest parts of the canal.

Going around Regent's Park you pass London Zoo, and a set of locks at Camden Town where there's a large market, lots of pubs and restaurants and a high-tech TV station with soft-boiled golden eggs in egg cups decorating the roof. Farther east, the canal skirts the edges of the City of London before cutting across the East End, past Victoria Park where it turns towards the Limehouse Basin and the Thames.

Regent's Canal towpath. Open daily, 9am–dusk.

Cutty Sark

If you want to see the greatest tea clipper ever, go down to Greenwich where the *Cutty Sark* is moored. Next to her is the *Gypsy Moth IV*, the ketch which Sir Francis Chichester sailed around the world single-handedly in 1967. See page 94 for details.

Historic Ships Collection

Moored in the East Basin of St Katherine Dock, near to Tower Bridge, is a collection of seven historic ships; a lightship, a coastal steamer, a Thames sailing barge, a tug, a herring drifter, a three-masted schooner and the RRS (stands for Royal Research Ship) *Discovery* that was used by Captain Scott as a headquarters ship on his first expedition to Antarctica. The ship had a tremendously strong double hull so that it could withstand being trapped in the ice for months at a time. The *Discovery* and all the rest of the ships can be boarded for a visit.

Next to the East Basin is a second marina where expensive private yachts are moored. You can't board them but there's nothing to stop you looking and dreaming. St Katherine Dock has lots of shops and restaurants to explore and it's fun to wander about here alongside the Thames.

Historic Ships Collection, St Katherine Dock, London E1. Open 10am–5pm. Admission £1.60 adults, £0.80 children.

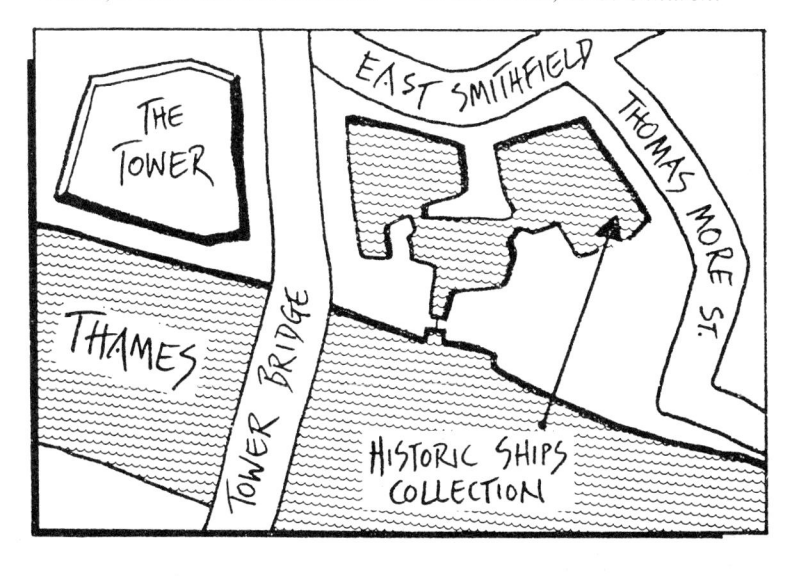

WATERWAYS

HMS Belfast

The only Royal Navy ship since HMS *Victory* to be preserved as a floating museum, this big gun cruiser last saw service in 1963. The *Belfast* was one of the biggest and most powerfully armed British ships ever; at sea she could hit moving targets up to 23 kilometres away. During World War II she was involved in the Battle of North Cape during which the *Scharnhorst* was sunk, and in 1944 was part of the fleet that bombarded the shores of Normandy just before the troops landed on D-Day.

Now she's permanently moored near Tower Bridge.

Visitors can board and explore most of her seven decks. You can clamber into two of the turrets that house her six-inch guns (in action it took 27 men to work each turret) and go from the Admiral's Bridge down to the messdecks where 800 sailors lived in the kind of crowded conditions you'd usually expect to find in a department store lift during a sale. You can go right through the crew's quarters, even viewing the bakery where bread for the *Belfast* and other ships in the fleet was prepared.

There's so much to see, say the museum staff, that you should allow yourself a good two hours to take it all in.

HMS Belfast, Symons Wharf, Vine Lane, Tooley Street, London SE1. Tel: 01-407 6434. Open daily, Mar–Oct 11am–5.50pm, Nov–Mar 11am–4.30pm. Admission £3.00 adults, £1.50 children.

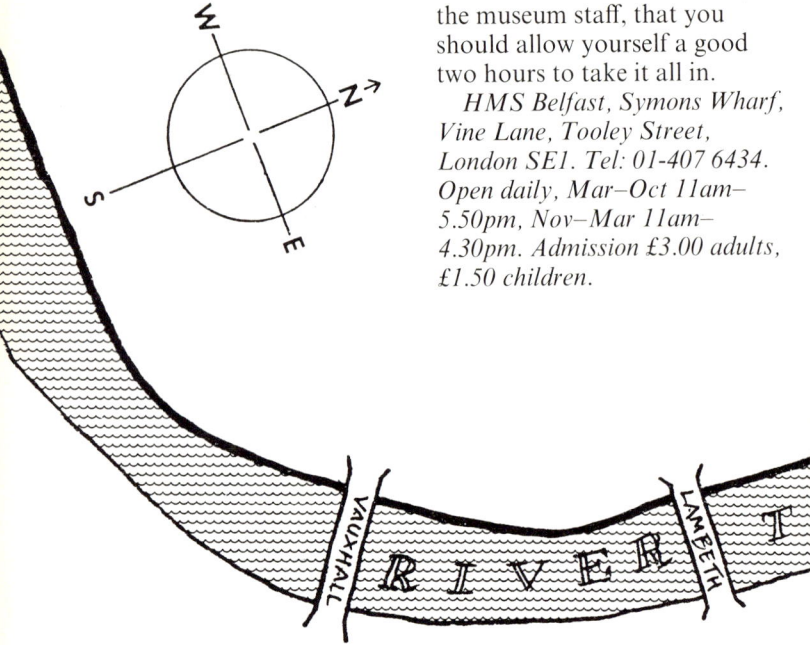

River Trips

From the centre of London at Westminster Pier or Charing Cross Pier there are a number of boat trips that you can take going either up or down the river. The cruises are accompanied by a commentary, which can be helpful if London landmarks don't mean all that much to you.

Upriver towards Kew, Richmond and Hampton Court the Thames seems to slow down and become everyone's favourite lazy river as it winds its way through pretty suburbs, where gardens slope to the river bank. Colonies of houseboats and countless moorings with punts, rowboats, small motorboats and sailing dingies line the riverbank. The opposite direction takes you past the City of London and Tower Bridge and along a wide river that was once a busy highway for ocean freighters – though the main docks have been moved much farther east, out of London to Tilbury. The cruise ships run down to Greenwich, past all the new buildings of the 'born-again' docklands. Some also continue as far as the Thames Barrier. Trips last anywhere from 30 minutes to three hours.

A number of river boats also run evening trips, or can be booked for lunch and supper cruises and evening discos. The main piers at which you can join and leave a cruise are:

Charing Cross Pier, Victoria Embankment, London WC2. Tel: 01-839 5393 for times and prices.

Greenwich Pier, Cutty Sark Gardens, London SE10. Tel: 01-858 3996 for times and prices.

Richmond Pier, Richmond Bridge, Richmond. Tel: 01-940 8505 for prices and times of sailings.

Tower Pier, Tower Hill, London EC3. Tel: 01-488 0344 for prices and times.

Westminster Pier, Victoria Embankment, London SW1. Tel: 01-930 4097 for sailings.

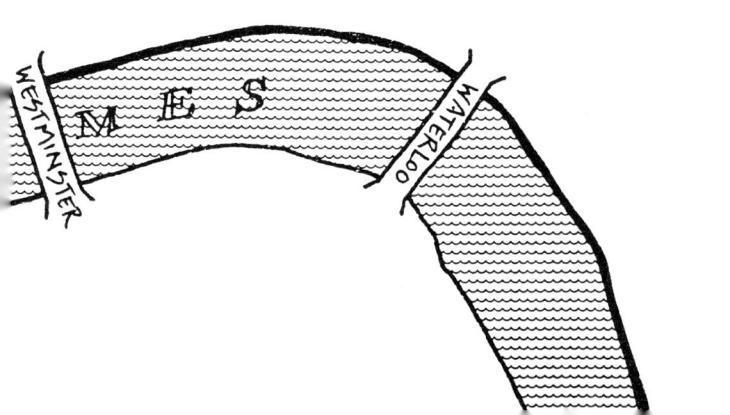

WATERWAYS

Schooner Kathleen & May

We always thought that a schooner was something you drank sherry out of until we discovered the kind that has masts and keels. The very last three-masted topsail schooner in Britain today is moored in the Thames immediately behind Southwark Cathedral. Once upon a time these ships were used everywhere as coastal freighters, ferrying cargoes of coal and other unromantic goods all around Britain and Ireland.

The *Kathleen & May*, now 85 years old, has been taken over and fully restored by the Maritime Trust, and these days can be visited by the public.

Schooner Kathleen & May, St Mary Overy Dock, Cathedral Street, London SE1. Open Mon–Fri 10am–5pm, Sat–Sun 11am–4pm. Admission £1.00 adults, £0.50 children.

Thames Barrier

The biggest moving flood barrier in the world can be found downstream from central London at Woolwich. It was completed in 1984 to protect London from freak high tides which might cause the Thames to break its banks and flood low-lying parts of town.

The Barrier consists of a series of gates (each one weighing 3700 tonnes) supported by a chain of nine great piers across the river. The floodgates lie flat on the river bed most of the time so that river traffic can pass over them. When a flood tide threatens they are raised into position, forming a wall of steel rising high above river level.

There's a Visitors' Centre here which has two films explaining how the barrier works and giving the facts and figures of its construction; there is also a working model that you can watch in action.

Thames Barrier, Unity Way, Woolwich, London SE18. Tel: 01-854 1373. Open daily 10.30am–5pm. Admission £1.00 adults, £0.50 children.

Wildlife

No, this isn't a section about the things that happen on the underground after 11pm when the pubs close; rather, it's all about the wild animals of London. Although people from time to time see mice wandering in tube stations, or are astonished by the number of pigeons and starlings that live around Trafalgar and Leicester Squares, the only genuinely interesting wildlife you're likely to see in London is in zoos, parks, farms and nature reserves. The rest of the place is given over mostly to cats, dogs and humans – three animal species that have developed the knack for driving just about everything else away.

Animal Enclosures

Lots of public parks in London have small animal sanctuaries off to one corner. Some of the creatures you'll see here are caged. Others, especially the birds, are more or less free to come and go as they please – though mostly they seem to take the attitude – why wander far from the food?

Parks, not mentioned elsewhere in this section, that have animal enclosures are:

Clissold Park, London N16 (ducks, geese, coots, swans, mynah birds, peacocks, cranes and deer).

Dulwich Park, London SE21 (has an aviary with toucans, budgies, motmots – said to nibble their tail feathers into a racquet shape – and others).

Golders Hill Park, London NW11 (geese and ducks, pheasants, deer, farm animals).

Holland Park, London W8 (peacocks, geese, pheasants, cranes and other birds).

Horniman Gardens, London SE23 (waterfowl and exotic birds).

Maryon Wilson Park, London SE7 (Chinese deer and sheep).

Regent's Park, London NW1 (lots and lots of waterfowl, many unusual species of duck, redstart, chiff chaff and others).

St James's Park, London SW1 (more than 20 kinds of ducks and geese, also pelicans).

Waterlow Park, London N6 (black swans, geese, ducks, quail, mynah birds, jays).

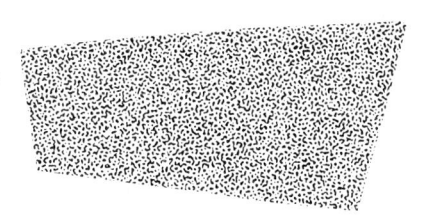

WILDLIFE

Battersea Park Children's Zoo

The one thing that marks a children's zoo from a grownup's is the size of its animals. Here at Battersea there's nothing behind bars that any self-respecting ten year-old can't look down on.

This mini-zoo has a deer enclosure, peacocks, parrots and guinea fowl, a pets corner with sheep and goats, and more than a barrel of monkeys – marmosets, black apes, a few lemurs – not to mention fennec foxes, otters and wallabies. There are pony rides too (costing 10p).

Battersea Park Children's Zoo, Battersea Park, London SW11. Tel: 01-871 7540. Open daily Easter–Oct, 11.30am–5.30pm. Admission free.

Brockwell Park

This little park was once the kitchen garden of a mansion in Stockwell, after which it was a flower garden. It still has many unusual trees and flowers, and a very old yew hedge. There is also a bird enclosure here where quail, toucans, jays and other birds are kept.

Brockwell Park, London SE24.

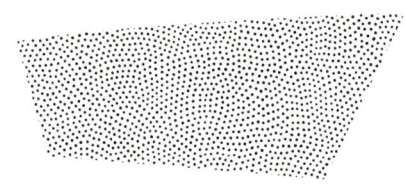

Chessington World of Adventure

What started life as a zoo has become a theme park with rides (Runaway Train, Dragon River, Fifth Dimension) and animals; you can still watch them minding their own business as you glide past overhead in the Safari Skyway monorail. The nice thing about this place is that for the price of a single admission you can visit everything there is to see.

Chessington World of Adventures, Leatherhead Road, Chessington, Surrey. Tel: 03727-27227. Open daily, April–Oct 10am–5pm, Nov–Mar 10am–4pm. Admission £3.75 adults, £2.00 children.

WILDLIFE

City Farms

A city farm is a way of reminding ourselves that milk doesn't only come from bottles, nor do jumpers grow ready-knitted in the wild.

In recent years close to 20 city farms have sprouted up on waste ground and abandoned sites all around London. The farms aim to give young people a chance to see what farm life is really like. You can go as a visitor, or else to get your hands dirty by helping to take care of the animals.

The Kentish Town City Farm is one of the more established ones. It has cows, horses, sheep, goats, pigs and poultry of all kinds. Children can touch and feed the animals, or help to muck out and clean their stables. On Sundays there are pony rides.

Another much bigger farm is Mudchute Park in docklands. There are 32 acres here, with pigs and sheep, cows, goats and fowl. There's also a pony club and a shop selling farm produce and refreshments.

Some of the most centrally located city farms are:

Freightliners Farm, Sheringham Road, Islington, London N7.

Kentish Town City Farm, 1 Cressfield Close, Grafton Road, London NW5.

Mudchute Park, Pier Street, Isle of Dogs, London E14.

Spitalfields Farm, c/o Thomas Buxton School, Buxton Street, London E1.

Surrey Docks Farm, Commercial Dock Passage, Gulliver Street, Rotherhithe, London SE16.

Vauxhall City Farm, 24 St Oswald's Place, London SE11.

WILDLIFE

Crystal Palace Children's Zoo

This little zoo in Crystal Palace Park keeps all the usual farm animals you'd expect (they wander about freely) and, for kids under 12 years, there's the chance to go on a pony ride too. It also has a good selection of unusual birds, like rheas, egrets, penguins, toucans and cranes, as well as monkeys and wallabies. It's a great place to get a close look at some unusual animals.

Children's Zoo, Crystal Palace Park, London SE20. Tel: 01-778 4487. Open Mon–Fri 1.30pm–5.30pm, Sat–Sun 1.30pm–6pm. Admission £0.40 adults, £0.20 children over three years.

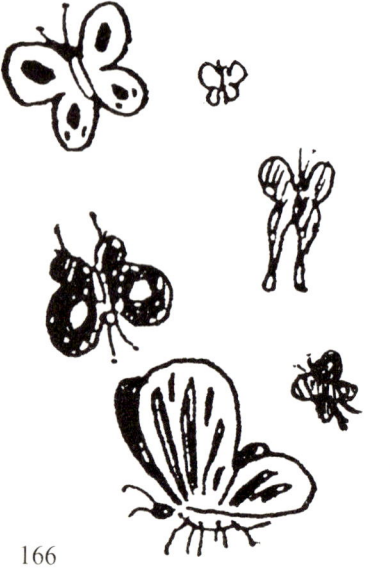

London Butterfly House

Inside a large greenhouse in Syon Park there's a tropical garden where visitors can go on a butterfly safari (pith helmets optional) to look at and identify as many different species as they can. The butterflies fly about freely and while you're here you may see amateur enthusiasts busily photographing them. As you wander through, look hard to see if you can find all the stages of their strange life cycle – egg to caterpillar to chrysalis and, finally, adult butterfly.

There's also an Insect Gallery where, if you peer hard among the foliage, you'll be able to spot live locusts, stick insects, leaf-cutter ants, scorpions and other insects, all safe behind a wall of glass.

London Butterfly House, Syon Park, Brentford, Middlesex. Tel: 01-560 7272. Open daily, Feb–Oct 10am–5pm, Nov–Feb 10am–3.30pm. Admission £1.80 adults, £1.00 children.

WILDLIFE

London Zoo

A huge zoo with over 8000 animals (though unlike Noah's Ark there are more than two of most species) – it has everything from tiger fish to tigers. There's a children's zoo and mock farmyard, a Moonlight World where you can stumble through the dark to peer at nocturnal animals, and chances to see animals being fed, bathed and milked. In the summertime there are pony and camel rides too.

London Zoo, Regent's Park, London NW1. Tel: 01-722 3333. Open daily Mar–Sept 9am–6pm, Oct–Feb 10am–dusk. Admission £3.60 adults, £1.80 children (under fives are free).

St Mary Magdelene Nature Reserve

Here, in an urban churchyard in east London, is an unspoiled pocket of wilderness where foxes, kestrels, owls and pheasants live, as well as small mammals like rabbits and mice, many kinds of insects and more than a dozen species of butterfly. All of these animals are native to London and would be perfectly at home here if you first got rid of the traffic, the pets and the people.

There's a nature trail that lets you wander through this 4-hectare reserve, and a small museum with an exhibition that helps to explain the ecology of the wildlife here (showing, for example, simple food chains).

St Mary Magdelene Nature Reserve, St Mary's Churchyard, Norman Road, East Ham, London E6. Tel: 01-470 4525. Open Mon–Fri 9am–5pm, Sat–Sun 2pm–5pm. Admission free.

Whipsnade Zoo

Strictly speaking this isn't a London site at all, though it's the nearest to London you could get a 200-hectare zoo. But Whipsnade is well worth the side-trip if you've got the time.

167

WILDLIFE

Its 2000 or so wild (but mostly not-so-wild) animals live in an open environment where they can roam about peacefully. You can't exactly pet the white rhinos, but you may be able to spot Przhewalski's Wild Horse (if not pronounce it), an early type of horse discovered in the late 1800s by a Russian explorer of the same name.

During summer months there is a full-gauge steam railway which runs around the zoo to let you take a closer look at the animals. Otherwise bring binoculars.

Whipsnade Park Zoo, Dunstable, Beds. Tel: 0582 872171. Open daily, 10am–dusk. Admission £3.20 adults, £1.60 children (under fives free). If you want to drive your car through the park there's an extra charge of £2.50.

Windsor Safari Park

Not far past Heathrow Airport, just outside the town of Windsor, is a large safari park. The safari idea is a simple one – put people in wheeled cages (cars) and let the animals run free. Here you drive along several different safari routes that take you past herds of lions, zebras, elephants, camels and giraffes, while on another route gangs of baboons will do everything but spray graffitti on your car. There's also a deer forest you can walk through, displays of tropical plants and butterflies and a terrific seaworld show – killer whales, dolphins and penguins doing their best to splash the humans. One admission ticket gets you into everything.

Windsor Safari Park, Windsor, Berks. Tel: 0753 869841. Open daily. Admission £5.50 adults, £4.50 children over four years.

WHO'S A PRETTY BOY THEN!

Sports & Outdoors

Even with the copious amount of detail in these pages you may find there's something missing – but never fear, help is just a phone call away. Dial *Sportsline* on 01-222 8000 and tell the friendly voice at the other end what your problem is and *voila!*, problem solved.

No, we didn't believe it was that easy either, so we phoned them up and asked about the most unlikely sport we could think of – Fives, as it happens – and a couple of minutes later the computer coughed up a contact phone number for both Rugby *and* Eton Fives! Our operator had never even heard of the game but it was lurking somewhere in the depths of their database anyway.

This is a totally free service that covers both sports you want to participate in and those you just want to watch, and includes every London borough as well as other areas if the sport is likely to have venues outside the city – like windsurfing and orienteering.

Archery

If you've a hankering to be a 20th century Robin Hood, or you're fed up with darts and want to try the long-distance version, there are plenty of places in and around London that offer you the chance to bend a bow. The following places all have facilities for beginners:

Aquarius Archers, Fortis Green Reservoir, junction of Southern & Lynmouth Roads, London N2. Nearest tube Finchley Central. Clubhouse Tel: 01-883 7212, club secretary Tel: 01-440 1558.

Brixton Recreation Centre, Brixton Road, London SW9. Tel: 01-274 7774. Beginners classes held every Wednesday, 6–8pm, £2.00 per session.

Cranford Community School, High Street, Cranford, Middlesex. Tel: 01-897 6609. Every Tuesday, between 6–8pm, an independent archery club holds classes for beginners. Fee charged.

SPORTS & OUTDOORS

Badminton

This, the gentle skill of whacking a shuttlecock to and fro, is a sport that looks deceptively easy. Don't be fooled, it's no sissy game and will certainly weed out the men from the boys who think it's oh so simple. The Badminton Association of England, Bradwell Road, Loughton Lodge, Milton Keynes, will supply you with more details than you'll care to know, but you can go down and play at:

Brixton Recreation Centre, Brixton Road, London SW9. Tel: 01-274 7774.

Crystal Palace National Sports Centre, Ledrington Road, London SE19. Tel: 01-778 0131.

Swiss Cottage Sports Centre, Winchester Road, London NW3. Tel: 01-586 5989.

Westminster Children's Sports Centre, Crompton Road, London W2. Tel: 01-258 3817.

Basketball

You might be forgiven for thinking that you have to be 2 metres tall, with feet like skis, to be able to play this game, but such is not the case – though if you're rather small and round of figure the big guys might well mistake you for the ball and bounce you. The British Association of Basketball, 26 Ickenham Close, West Ruislip, Middlesex (Tel: 08956 73955), will supply all the details, but here are a selection of London venues:

London Central YMCA, 112 Great Russell Street, London WC2. Tel: 01-637 8131.

London School of Basketball, Moberly Centre, Kilburn Lane, London W10. Tel: 01-960 2336.

Michael Sobell Sports Centre, Hornsey Road, London N7. Tel: 01-607 1632.

SPORTS & OUTDOORS

Canoeing

Canoes these days would not be recognized by the first, let alone the last of the Mohicans – the nearest these sleek fibreglass constructions get to trees is the ones they pass on the river bank. But if your idea of a great time is getting dunked in cold running water here are some places that'll supply the wherewithall – provided you can swim, of course.

Islington Boat Club, 16–34 Graham Street, London N18. Tel: 01-253 0778.

Pirate Club, Pirate Castle, Oval Road, Camden Town, London NW1. Tel: 01-267 6605. Accepts non-members.

South East London Aquatic Centre, Woolwich Dockyard, Woolwich Church Street, London SE18. Tel: 01-855 0131. Accepts non-members.

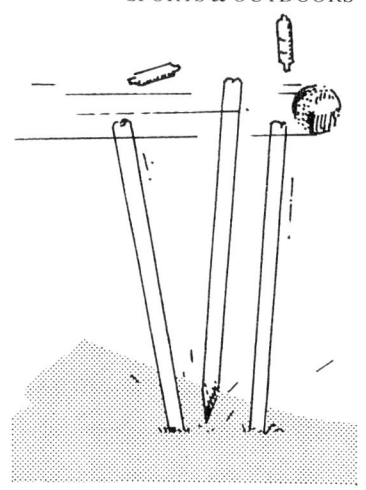

Cricket

An American dictionary we have defines cricket as 'a popular outdoor game, played with two sides of eleven each, with bats, ball, and wickets'. Would that it were that simple! Our own definition might be legalised insane behaviour, particularly if it's a bad summer, but if you're keen on participating or watching contact:

Grover Cricket School, 172 East Hill, London SW18. Tel: 01-874 1796.

Islington Recreation Dept., Wray Crescent, London N4. Tel: 01-607 7331.

Waltham Forest's Britannia Sports Ground, Billet Road, London E17. Tel: 01-521 7111.

During the season (May–Sept) check newspapers for Test Match venues.

SPORTS & OUTDOORS

Cycling

Getting on a bike and riding around central London is as close as you're ever likely to get to dicing with death – if the roads don't get you the drivers will, sooner or later. The British Cycle Federation, 16 Upper Woburn Place, London WC1 (Tel: 01-387 9320), will give you information about touring, and the following places have cycle tracks:

Crystal Palace National Sports Centre, Ledrington Road, London SE19. Tel: 01-788 0131.

Eastway Cycle Circuit, Leyton. Tel: 01-519 0017.

You can, if you have a permit, cycle along canal towpaths. Contact British Waterways Board on their Canalphone. Tel: 01-723 8486.

Dance

If you get the terpsichoreal urge all of a sudden, and have no idea how to deal with it, we're here to help – it simply means you want to get up and dance. If this ever happens, here are some places where you can cut loose.

Battersea Arts Centre, Lavender Hill, London SW11. Tel: 01-223 6557.

Dance Centre, 12 Floral Street, Covent Garden, London WC2. Tel: 01-836 6544.

Pineapple Dance Centre, 7 Langley Street, London WC2. Tel: 01-836 4004.

Royal Academy of Dancing, 48 Vicarage Crescent, London SW11. Tel: 01-223 0091.

SPORTS & OUTDOORS

Fishing

This is as good a way to waste time as anything we've ever come across, and now that the Thames is somewhat cleaner, and less like the open sewer it once was, you now have an even chance of actually catching something in it – apart from a bad cold if you happen to fall in. In and around London there are also various ponds and reservoirs where you can fish, although some places require permits.

Barn Elms Reservoir, Merthyr Terrace, London SW13. Tel: 01-748 3423. Permit required.

Crystal Palace Boating Lake, London SE19. Tel: 01-778 7148. Permit required.

Grand Union Canal, c/o London Anglers Association, 183 Hoe Street, London E17. Tel: 01-520 7477. Permit required.

Battersea Park, Epping Forest Ponds, Hampstead Heath and Highgate Ponds, Wandsworth Common and many others do not require permits.

Football

When a country's national game turns into an international disgrace it's hardly the time to recommend it to visitors. Sadly, this is the case with football. There are a lot of grounds where you take your life in your hands when you go to watch a match, but the Football Association are trying their hardest to put matters to rights. We can't really give an absolute seal of approval to any of the major London grounds – if you want to watch football, 'you pays yer money', as they say, 'and you takes yer chances'.

If you want to play, on the other hand, almost all the sports centres listed elsewhere in this section can help, or simply take a walk around the nearest park and try and join in a game!

SPORTS & OUTDOORS

Golf

Every sport has a language all its own, but golf-speak has to be one of the weirdest. Certain shots are called *birdies* and others *eagles*, and various clubs are referred to as *mashie* and *nibblick*; well, the game was invented in Scotland...

If you want to play a round or two you'll have to contact a golf course – of which there are, surprisingly, a bewildering number in the general London area. Better to go to your nearest bookshop and get hold of a copy of Donald Steele's *Guide to the Golf Courses of Great Britain*, published by the Daily Telegraph. This book lists all available courses, and tells you which ones are open to the public.

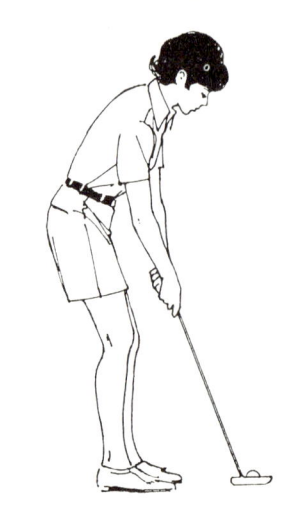

Ice-skating

A well-padded rear end really comes into its own when starting out with this particular activity – as more time is spent falling on it than not. Most rinks will hire you a pair of skates at a very reasonable price, certainly much cheaper than buying your own!

Lea Valley Ice Centre, Lea Bridge Road, London E10. Tel: 01-533 3151.

Queen's Ice-skating Club, Queensway, London WC2. Tel: 01-229 0172.

Richmond Ice Rink, Clevedon Road, Twickenham, Middlesex. Tel: 01-893 3646.

Michael Sobell Sports Centre, Hornsey Road, London N7. Tel: 01-607 1632.

Streatham Ice Rink, 386 Streatham High Road, London SW16. Tel: 01-769 7861.

Martial Arts

When it comes to the various ways you can yell *HAIII-YAA!!* and cleave the air with a vicious chop of your hand you really are spoilt for choice. There's everything from Aikido to Tai Chi Chuan. Each discipline has its own association, and we recommend you call them and find out what's available. Generally speaking these activities are not the sort of thing to take lightly – without guidance they are dangerous.

British Aikido Association, 331 Old Farm Avenue, Sidcup, Kent. Tel: 01-302 9307.

British Ju-jitsu Association, c/o R. Morris, 16 Bexley Gardens, Edmonton, London N9. Tel: 01-254 5682.

British Judo Association, 16 Upper Woburn Place, London WC1. Tel: 01-387 9340.

Amateur Karate Association, 80 Judd Street, London WC1. Tel: 01-837 4406.

British Kung Fu Association, c/o R. M. Bull & Co., Oakdale Avenue, Northwood, Middlesex. Tel: 09274 20808.

British Tai Chi Chuan Association, 7 Wimpole Street, London W1. Tel: 01-935 8444.

SPORTS & OUTDOORS

Roller skating

Ice skating without ice is probably the best way to describe this precursor to skateboarding and street hockey. There are very few places set up specifically for it, but why not try:

Westbourne Green Sports Centre, Torquay Street, London W2. Tel: 01-798 3707.

Skateboarding

If you happen to have packed your skateboard, just in case, here are two places where you can surf a public footpath out of reach of marauding cars:

Meanwhile Gardens, Elkstone Road, London W10.

South Bank Complex, underneath Queen Elizabeth Hall, Belvedere Road, London SE1.

Riding

Once you've overcome any fears you might have about sitting on something as large and fast as a horse, riding one is a breeze. It's the next morning that it becomes a pain in the backside. For your information *hacking* is going out and having a good time, while *riding* is doing it properly, according to the lady at the Bathurst Stables! Here are three places where you can hire horses or take classes in riding:

Bathurst Riding Stables, 63 Bathurst Mews, London W2. Tel: 01-723 2813.

Lea Bridge Riding School, Lea Bridge Road, London E10. Tel: 01-556 2629.

Trent Park Equestrian Centre, Bramley Road, Southgate, London N14. Tel: 01-363 9630.

SPORTS & OUTDOORS

Tennis

For all you aspiring Borgs, Beckers and Cash's out there we have just one word of advice for you – practise. You can do this at:

Hammersmith Park, South Africa Road, London W12.

Bishops Park, Stevenage Road, London SW6.

Westbourne Green Sports Centre, Torquay Street, London W2. Tel: 01-798 3703.

Lawn Tennis Association, Falliser Road, London W14. Tel: 01-385 2366 for all information about clubs and coaching.

Swimming

We've always thought that swimming in a pool is far and away more preferrable to attempting the same in the sea – mainly because the water's warmer (we're only talking about indoor pools here) and there's absolutely no sand. There are local swimming pools all around London, but you can swim in central London at:

Chelsea Sports Centre, Chelsea Manor Street, London SW3. Tel: 01-352 6985.

Dolphin Square Sports Centre, Chichester Street, London SW1. Tel: 01-828 1618.

Marshall Street Baths, Marshall Street, off Carnaby Street, London W1. Tel: 01-437 7665.

Oasis, Endell Street, Covent Garden, London WC2. Tel: 01-836 9555.

Water-slides

These places allow you to experience what it's like to be the bath water once the plug's been pulled. If this sounds like your kind of fun, either see a doctor or go to:

Big Zippa, White City Pool, Bloemfontein Road, London W12. Tel: 01-743 3401.

Big Splash, King George's Park, London SW18. Tel: 01-870 4955. Open only during May–Sept.

Wild Waters, next to Richmond Swimming Baths, Old Deer Park, Richmond, Surrey. Tel: 01-948 8853.

Classes & Clubs

You can keep busy forever by going to clubs or classes in London. Or, if you have a favourite hobby and want to find out where to go to meet other enthusiasts, the first thing to do is ring *Kidsline*. It's a free information service with a huge file of data on just about every kids' activity in London. Want to make a film? Take classes in magic? Learn to jazz dance? Throw a pot? *Kidsline* is bound to have the answer.

There's also a 24-hour recorded message service called *Children's London*. You'll be able to listen to details of the current week's events for children – theatre, festivals, clubs, shows, and so forth. Indispensable.

Children's London. Tel: 01-246 8007. Open daily 24 hours.
Kidsline. Tel: 01-222 8070. Mon–Fri 4pm–6pm, school holidays 9am–4pm.

Arts & Crafts

If you develop a sudden urge to take up pottery, painting, puppet making, sculpting or woodwork there are plenty of arts and crafts centres that run weekend and school holiday classes for children.

Camden Arts Centre, Arkwright Road, London NW3. Tel: 01-435 2643.

Camden Institute, 87 Holmes Road, London NW5. Tel: 01-267 1414.

Central YMCA, 112 Great Russell Street, London WC1. Tel: 01-637 8131.

Chelsea Pottery, 13 Radnor Walk, London SW3. Tel: 01-352 1366.

Horniman Museum (Saturday craft club), Forest Hill, London SE23. Tel: 01-699 2339.

Astronomy Classes

If you are over eight years old and are hooked on the idea of finding out more about the planets and stars why not drop in on the monthly Saturday morning classes run by Morley College.

Family Astronomy Classes, Morley College, Westminster Bridge Road, London SE1. Tel: 01-928 8501.

Brass Rubbing

When medieval bigwigs were buried they were not content with being remembered solely by a simple gravestone. A more lasting memorial, in the shape of a highly detailed picture of themselves, often accompanied by wife and/or dog, was created in brass and fixed to the top of their tombs.

Today it is possible to make copies of these brasses by laying a sheet of heavy paper over them and rubbing with a wax crayon. It's easy to do, and you get a beautiful copy of the brass to take home with you.

London Brass Rubbing Centre, St James's Church, Piccadilly, London W1. Tel: 01-437 6023. Open Mon–Sat 10am–6pm. Sun 12 noon–6pm. Charge for rubbing materials.

All-Hallows-By-The-Tower, Byward Street, London EC3. Tel: 01-481 2928. Open Mon–Sat 11am–5.00pm. Sun 12.30pm–5.00pm. Charge for rubbing materials.

The Brass Rubbing Centre, Westminster Abbey, London SW1. Tel: 01-222 2085. Open Mon–Sat 9am–5.30pm. Charge for rubbing materials.

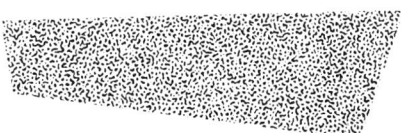

CLASSES & CLUBS

Chess Clubs

Lots of chess associations have classes for junior members, which in some cases means anyone over seven years old. As long as you know the basic moves you'll find people here who can teach you the strategies to help you to improve your game.

Canada Villa Youth Centre, Pursley Road, London NW7 (meets Tuesdays 5.30pm–8pm). Tel: 01-959 2811.

London Central YMCA, 112 Great Russell Street, London WC1 (meets Sundays 4pm–6.30pm). Tel: 01-637 8131.

Getting On Stage

If you fancy learning a bit about acting or mime, or having a go at clowning, magic tricks or circus acrobatics you can go to classes at several places in London.

Clown Alley, Churchill Theatre, High Street, Bromley, Kent. Tel: 01-460 6677. Workshops Sat 2pm–3pm.

Davenports Magic Classes, Charing Cross Shopping Arcade, Strand, London WC2. Tel: 01-836 0408. Saturday morning magic classes.

Polka Workshops, Polka Children's Theatre, 240 The Broadway, Wimbledon, London SW19. Tel: 01-543 3741. Saturdays and school holidays.

Unicorn Club Workshops, Great Newport Street, London WC2. Tel: 01-379 3280. Saturdays and school holidays.

CLASSES & CLUBS

Making Music

There are so many places where you can go to learn to make music that it's more of a problem choosing an instrument than where to be taught. Here are a few centres that run music classes and workshops.

Battersea Arts Centre, (music workshop for parents and kids). Tel: 01-223 8413.

Greenwich Young People's Theatre, (rock music workshop for kids 14+). Tel: 01-855 4911.

London College of Music, (Saturday junior music school for kids 10+). Tel: 01-437 6120.

Morley College, (Saturday morning family music workshops). Tel: 01-928 8501.

Youth Music Centre, (Saturday music school for children), Bigwood House School, Bigwood Road, London NW11. Tel: 01-907 8018.

Index

Page numbers in italics refer to illustrations.

A

Acting 180
Airports 92
Albany Empire 135
Alexandra Palace & Park 148
Animal enclosures 163
Anne Boleyn 56, *57*
Archery 169
Arts and crafts 178
Astronomy classes 179
Athletics 83

B

Badminton 170
Baker Street Station 11
Balloons 118
Bank of England 42, *43*
Bankside 34
Barbican Children's Cinema 142, 144
Barristers *44*, 45
Basketball 170
Battersea Arts Centre 135, 142
Battersea Park 148
Battersea Park Children's Zoo 164
Battle of Britain Week 90
Beatties 118
Beefeaters *22*, 56
Bernigra's 129
Bethnal Green Museum of Childhood 106
Big Ben 24
Billingsgate Market 36, 48, 118
Birdlife *72*, 73
Blackheath 149
Boats to hire 157
Bond Street Station 10
Bookshops 119
Boxing 83
Brass rubbing 86, 179
Bridges *30*, 31
British Motor Museum 106
British Museum 61, 107
Brockwell Park 164
Buckingham Palace 20, *21*
Buses *12–13*, 16, 17
Bushey Park 149
Buskers 139

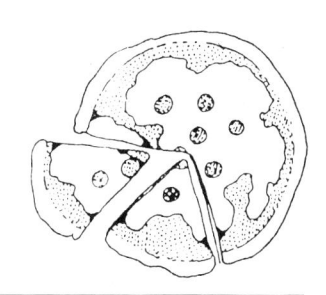

C

Cabaret Mechanical Theatre 92
Cabinet War Rooms 107
Cakes and pastries 129
Camden Lock Market 119
Camping Gear 119
Canals *38–39*
Canal trips 157
Canal walks 158
Canoeing 171
Carnaby Street 120
Cat Show 91
Changing of the Guard *21*, 93
Chelsea Physic Garden 150
Chess clubs 180
Chessington World of
   Adventures 164
Chinese New Year 88
Christmas 91
City Farms 75, 165
City of London 40–49
City police *40*
Clarence House 28
Cleopatra's Needle *34*
Clown's Church Service 88

Columbia Road Market 120
Comics 120
Commonwealth Institute 108
Computers 121
Concerts for children 140–141
Coronation 67
Costumes 121
Cricket *83*, 171
Crown Jewels 22
Croydon Warehouse 135
Cruft's Dog Show *88*
Crystal Palace 84–85
Crystal Palace Children's Zoo
   166
Crystal Palace Park 71, 75, 149
Cutty Sark 94, 159
Cycling 83, 172

D

Dance 172
Deep Pan Pizza Company 129
Deer 73
Diamond Centre 94
Dina's Diner 129

Dinosaurs *60, 71*
Doggett's Coat and Badge Race 90
Dogs' Cemetery 95
Doll's House 121

E

Easter Parade 88
Elizabeth II *18*, 19
Embankment 34
Express Dairy tour 95

F

Fast food 130
Films 142–143
Fire brigades 89
Fish and chips 130
Fishing *84–85*, 173
Flamsteed House 87
Fleet Street 80

Football *82–83*, 89, 173
Football Club tours 95
Ford Motor Company tour *81*, 96
Fortnum & Mason Soda Fountain 130
Free entertainment 144–145
Friary Court 28
Fun with Music 141

G

Games 122
Garfunkel's 130
Gatwick Airport 92
Geales 130
Geffrye Museum 108
Geological Museum 108
Gifts 122
Glasshouse 96
Golf 174
Great Fire 36, 48, 65
Greenwich Royal Observatory 87
Guided Tours 16–17

Guided Walks 155
Guinness World of Records 97
Gypsy Moth IV 94

H

Hamleys 122, 131
Hampstead Heath 69, 70, 150
Hampton Court *29*, 151
Harrods Ice Cream Parlour 131
Heathrow Airport 16, 92
Henry VIII 28, 29, 56
Highwaymen 50–51
Historic Ships Collection 159
HMS *Belfast 37*, 160
Hobbies 178–181
Holland Park 151
Horniman Museum 109
Horse Guards 26
Household Cavalry *26–27*
Hyde Park 71, 151
Hyper-Hyper 123

I

ICA Children's Cinema Club 142
Ice-cream 131
Ice-skating 174
Imperial War Museum 110
Independent Broadcasting Authority Museum 97

J

Jokes, Tricks & Magic 123

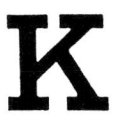

K

Kensington Market 123
Kew Bridge Steam Museum 110
Kew Gardens *70*, 152
Kites 68, *69*, 124

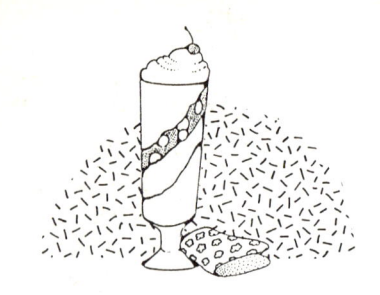

L

La Maison des Sorbets 132
Lauderdale Arts Centre 135
Law Courts 44, 45, 91
Leadenhall Market *43*, 124
Lincoln's Inn Fields 54
Little Angel Marionette Theatre 135
Lloyd's of London 98
London Bridge 35
London Butterfly House 154, 166
London Dungeon 98
London Fire Brigade Museum 111
London Planetarium 99
London Toy & Model Museum 111
London Transport Museum 112
London Zoo *74–75*, 167
Lord Mayor's Show *41*, 91
Lords Cricket Ground 83, 99
Lunchtime concerts 140
Lyons Corner House 132
Lyric Theatre 136

M

MacDonald's 132
Madame Tussaud's 100
Magic Moment 132
Magic tricks 180
Maison Bertaux 133
Maison Bouquillon 133
Maps *2–3, 8, 14, 30–31, 40, 46, 77, 78, 92–93*
Marine Ices 133
Markets 124
Martial Arts 175
Meridian Building 87
Mime 180
Mithras *87*
Model shops 124
Molecule Theatre of Science 136
Morley College Family Concerts 141
Mudlarks 33
Museum of Garden History 112
Museum of London 65, 113
Museum of Mankind 113
Music & concerts 139–141
Musical instruments 125

Music, playing 181
My Old Dutch 133

N

National Army Museum 113
National Film Theatre 143
National Maritime Museum 114
National Portrait Gallery *62*
National Theatre 101, 136, 144
National Westminster Tower *49*
Natural History Museum 60, 114
Nelson's Column *6*
New Caledonian Market 125
New Covent Garden 126
Newspaper tours 100
Nightingale, Florence 26, *62*
North London Link *78–79*
Notting Hill Carnival *90*

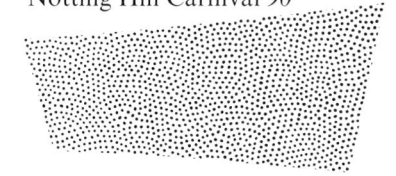

O

Old Bailey 44, 51
Old Curiosity Shop *54*, 55
Old St Thomas Operating Theatre 115
Open Air Art 144
Orange Tree Theatre 137
Owls 60
Oxford and Cambridge Boat Race *30*, 88

P

Palace Guards 20
Palace of Westminster *24–25*
Pappagalli's Pizza 134
Parliament *24–25*
Parks 148–154
Pearly Kings and Queens *91*
Pepys, Samuel *47*, 65
Performing meals 133
Petticoat Lane 126

Pizza 133
Pizza Express 134
Pizza Pasta Factory 134
Planetarium *86–87*, 99
   Greenwich 87
Polka Children's Theatre 137
Pollock's Toy Museum 64, 115
Pool of London 36
Porters 134
Portobello Road 126
Postboxes *19*
Posters 127
Post Office 80
Post Office tours 101
Post Office Tower *7*
Prime Minister 8, 24, *55*
Proms, last night of, 90
Public Record Office 79
Puffing Billy *58*
Punch and Judy shows 145
Puppet Theatre Barge 137

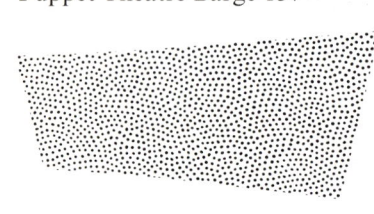

Q

Queen's Gallery 21
Queen Victoria 19, 29

R

Railway stations *14–15*, 35
Records 127
Regent's Canal *38*
Regent's Park 74, 153
Richmond 79
Richmond Park 70, 73, 153
Riding *85*, 176
Riverside Studios 137
River Thames 16, *17, 23*, 30, 31, 32, *35, 36–37*, 79
River trips 161
Roller skating 176
Romans 30, 40, 87
Roman wall 46–47
Royal Airforce Museum 116
Royal Courts of Justice 45, 91

Royal Exchange 42
Royal Festival Hall 141
Royal International Horse
   Show 90, *91*
Royal Mews 21
Royal Opera House 102

S

Sadler's Wells Theatre 138
St Bride's Church 34
St Dunstan's-in-the-East 48
St Georges Theatre 138
St James's Palace *28–29*
St James's Park 154
St Katherine Dock *33*, 159
St Mary Magdelene Nature
   Reserve 167
St Olave's Church 47
St Paul's Cathedral 34, *66*, 103
Saturday morning cinema clubs
   143
Schooner *Kathleen & May* 162
Science Museum 58, 116
Screen on the Hill 143

Selfridges Basement & Top of
   the Shop 135
Sheep Dog Trials 89
Show jumping 83
Silver Jubilee Walk 156
Skateboarding 176
Skiing 85
Smithfield Market 40, 127
Smollensky's Balloon 135
Sobell Sports Centre 84, 85
Speaker's Corner *71*, 145
Special Cinemas 143
Spitalfields Market 128
Sports 169–177
Stamps 68, 128
Street markets *76–77*
Swan Upping 90
Swimming 177
Syon Park 154

T

Tate Gallery 116
Telecom Technology Showcase
   117

Telephones, public 9
Tennis *83*, 177
Texas Lone Star Saloon 135
Thames flood barrier *31*, 162
The L.A. Cafe 136
The Monument 36, *48*, 49
The Satellite Cafe 136
The Seashell 136
Theatre Museum 117
Thieves *52–53*
Tomb of the Unknown Warrior 67
Tottenham Court Road Station 73
Tower Bridge *23, 36–37*
Tower Hill Station 46
Tower of London 22, 23, 56, 57
Toy Museum 111, 115
Toys *68–69*
Trent Park 154
Tricycle Theatre 138
Trooping the Colour *26*, 89
Tube map *2–3*
TV Show Visits 103
Twickenham Football Ground 104
Tyburn *50–51*

U

Unicorn Theatre 138

V

Valerie's 136
Victoria Embankment Gardens 32
Views 155
Vintage Car Run 91

W

Walks 155–156
War planes 59
Waterbus *38–39*
Watergate *32*
Waterloo Bridge 34

Watermans Art Centre 138
Water-slides 177
Wembley Market 128
Wendy Restaurants 136
Westminster Abbey 66, 67, 104
Whipsnade Zoo 167
Whirligig Theatre 139
Whitbread Stables 105
Wigs, lawyers 45
Wildlife *72–73*, 163–168
William the Conqueror 22, 56
Wimbledon Tennis
 Championship *83*, 89
Windsor Safari Park 168
Wood Museum 70
Wren, Christopher 34, 48, 66

Y

Young Vic 139

Z

Zoos, *see* Battersea Park
 Children's Zoo; Crystal
 Palace Children's Zoo;
 London Zoo; Whipsnade
 Zoo; Windsor Safari Park

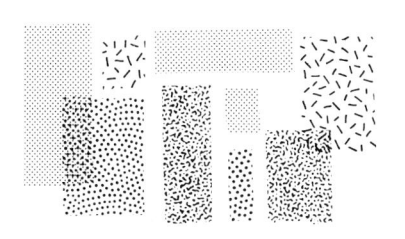

Acknowledgements
The publishers wish to thank the following people and organizations who have supplied illustrations for this book:

Avon Rubber Company
Bank of England
British Museum
British Tourist Authority
British Waterways Board
Central Office of Information
Coloursport
Department of the Environment
Ford Motor Company
GLC Print Collection
London Docklands Development Corporation
London Transport
Mansell Collection
Mick Alexander/Capital Press
Museum of London
National Portrait Gallery
National Westminster Bank
Ordnance Survey
Peter Abbey/Camera Press
Property Services Agency
Sportsimage
Whitbread Brewery
ZEFA
Zoological Society of London